VIDEO POKER

PLAY LONGER WITH LESS RISK

Carol Costa

ECW Press

Disclaimer

The gambling strategies and suggestions in this book are based solely on the experiences and opinions of the author. No guarantees are made or implied with regard to use of the information contained herein.

Published by ECW PRESS
2120 Queen Street East, Suite 200, Toronto, Ontario, Canada M4E 1E2

NATIONAL LIBRARY OF CANADA CATALOGUING IN PUBLICATION DATA

Costa, Carol
Video poker : play longer with less risk / Carol Costa.

ISBN 1-55022-592-8

1. Video poker. I. Title.

GV1469.35.P65C68 2003 795.41'2'0285 C2003-902201-3

Cover and Text Design: Tania Craan
Layout: Tania Craan
Printing: Transcontinental

This book is set in AG Round and Minion

DISTRIBUTION
CANADA: Jaguar Book Group, 100 Armstrong Avenue, Georgetown, ON, L7G 5S4

UNITED STATES: Independent Publishers Group, 814 North Franklin Street, Chicago, Illinois 60610

EUROPE: Turnaround Publisher Services, Unit 3, Olympia Trading Estate, Coburg Road, Wood Green, London N2Z 6T2

AUSTRALIA AND NEW ZEALAND: Wakefield Press, 1 The Parade West (Box 2066), Kent Town, South Australia 5071

PRINTED AND BOUND IN CANADA

ECW PRESS
ecwpress.com

Contents

INTRODUCTION

As a young girl growing up in Chicago, I walked to the bus stop every evening to meet my grandfather as he returned home from his downtown office. On the corner where I waited for him, there was a newsstand run by a man named Benny.

Eventually, Benny and I became friends. Often he asked me to watch the newspaper stand while he slipped into the drugstore to make a quick phone call. I thought watching the newsstand was quite an important assignment, but after a while I became curious about why Benny had to run off and make so many phone calls. My grandfather explained that Benny was a bookie and that the phone calls he made were to place bets on horses for some of his regular customers.

Although I wasn't old enough to place any wagers, one evening I asked Benny just how this betting thing worked.

"There's only one thing you need to know about gambling, little lady," Benny whispered gruffly. "If you're going to bet, play the favorite to show."

It was years before I understood what Benny had told me, much less put his advice to the test.

Then one night my friends and I went to a local racetrack to see the harness races. It was there I learned what the "favorite" was and that there was one in every race. I also learned that you could bet a horse to win, place, or show.

By that time, Benny himself was nothing more than a blurred image in my memory bank, but suddenly his words rang in my ears. "Play the favorite to show." More importantly, the words now made sense. I bet the favorite to show in each race. While some of my friends went home broke, I walked away with all my own money and some of the racetrack's money too.

Over the years, I became more and more of a gambler. Moving west, I made frequent trips to Las Vegas and Laughlin, Nevada. Now with Indian gaming, there are four casinos in my hometown and dozens of others in adjacent areas. Although Benny's advice was meant for horse racing, I have found that his method can be adapted to other casino games.

Playing the favorite to show is not a guaranteed way to win. There is no method that will allow you to win every time; if there were, there wouldn't be any racetracks or casinos.

Also, this low-key method is not for the "high rollers." They risk big money and expect to get large returns. The casinos give them nice perks — such as free rooms and meals — for playing in their establishments. Why do the casinos do that? Because the odds are in the casino's favor, and when the high roller loses, the casino realizes a nice profit in exchange for the complimentary accommodations extended to the gambler.

The purpose of this book is to show you how to keep playing with the least amount of risk. It is not for the high roller but for the conservative gambler who enjoys the games and social contact. You will probably not get rich playing this way, but the longer you are able to stay in the game, the more the odds turn in your favor.

Some games don't fit easily into this method of getting the most out of your wager. However, this moderate approach works well for one of the most popular casino games, video poker.

Most casinos offer an enticing array of video poker machines. This book will explain the basics of the game and discuss some of the flashy variations designed to make video poker more appealing to the average person. More importantly, this book will show you how to play the favorite to show to meet the challenges of video poker in a way that will increase your playing time and your chances of walking away a winner.

CHAPTER 1

Casino Poker Games

An elderly woman slid onto the stool in front of the video poker machine next to me. She inserted a $20 bill into the currency slot on the front of the machine and watched it slide out of sight. A few seconds later, the machine clicked its acceptance of her bill and registered 80 credits on the screen.

"What do I do now?" the woman asked the man standing next to her.

He shrugged. "I think you have to make a bet first."

The woman pushed the button marked maximum bet, and her credits were instantly reduced by five. It was a quarter poker machine, so she had just placed a bet for $1.25. Within seconds, her first poker hand appeared on the screen in front of her.

"Now what?" the woman asked her companion.

"Hold something," he replied.

"What should I hold?"

Both of them studied the cards on the screen. "You've got a possible straight, hold the eight, ten, jack, and queen," the man finally decided.

The woman obediently pushed the hold buttons in front of those cards. "Now what?"

"Push deal."

The computer took away the card she didn't hold and replaced it with another. Unfortunately, the new card wasn't a nine and didn't fit into the hand she was playing. No straight, no win.

Although I was occupied with my own video poker game, I continued to eavesdrop on the elderly couple. I was tempted to offer some advice, but the man seemed to understand the game, so I kept quiet.

In less than five minutes, the credits on the woman's machine were gone. She had lost her $20.

"I don't like this game," she said as she pushed herself off the stool. "It took the last of my money."

"Because you don't know how to play poker," he said, as if he hadn't been advising her on every hand she lost.

"You know how to play," she retorted. "So how come we lost?"

I smiled. She wasn't going to let him off the hook too easily.

"Machines are different than playing with people," he responded defensively.

Then they walked away and were swallowed up by the noise and congestion of the crowded casino.

I silently agreed with him. Playing video poker machines is a lot different than sitting around a table playing with real people.

Having grown up in a large, boisterous, Italian family, I was quite familiar with the basic game of poker. Every family gathering with my relatives included a poker game sandwiched between the main meal and dessert. Once you were old enough to reach the table without a booster chair, you were allowed to play.

My grandfather had a huge jar filled with pennies and acted as the banker. At the end of the game, all of us cashed our pennies back in to ensure their availability for the next game. My sisters thought the pennies could be put to better use at the candy store and never played poker, but I loved to play.

I started out sitting next to my father or one of the other adults so they could watch my hand and advise me. Once I mastered the poker terms, and learned that three of a kind, even three twos, beat a pair of aces, I was on my own.

Of course, the family games were filled with good-natured arguments and a fair amount of bluffing and cheating. I thought they were the best fun a girl could have.

We took turns dealing the cards for each hand, and the dealer got to make up the rules for that hand. "Five-card stud, no wild card," the dealer would say as he or she distributed the cards. "Seven-card draw, one-eyed kings are wild," the next dealer would announce as the players threw their pennies into the pot for another game. Then there was a game called Baseball. Threes and nines were wild, and four was a free card.

When it was my turn, I always called for five-card draw, jacks or better, to open. All these years later, I'm still playing that game — only now, instead of sitting around my dining room table with relatives who were often kind enough to fold on three of a kind so that my pair of aces could take the pennies in the pot, I am pitting my skills against a computer.

Playing video poker machines is indeed different. The computer always deals, you're the only one who bets, and your hand is the only one being played. It calls for a whole new understanding of the game, for a different mind-set and strategy.

You can't raise your bet after the first five cards have been dealt. The amount you receive for a winning hand is predetermined by a handy chart displayed on the machine.

There is no bluffing. You have the cards that appear on the screen and can't pretend to have something else. You hold and draw. If you don't come up with jacks or better, you lose your bet. A single pair of jacks or better will only pay the amount you just bet on that hand. The machine can't bluff you either, nor can it slip an ace up its sleeve, but that doesn't mean it can't take your money faster than Superman streaking across the sky to save Lois Lane.

Like the elderly couple who played beside me at the casino, you can lose $20 in five minutes or less if you don't know how to bet and play against a computer. While the basic rules of the game haven't changed, there are differences that require planning.

Video poker is a form of entertainment. You should put it in the same category as movies, stage plays, concerts, cable television, and many other things you pay for that bring you enjoyment and take your mind off the everyday problems of life.

What sets casino gaming apart from all other types of amusement is the underlying possibility that the money spent there could be returned to you 100 times over. The walls of casinos are often lined with photographs of smiling people who have hit big jackpots. With a little luck, it could happen to anyone, and that is why the casinos attract people from all walks of life.

Like all gamblers, video poker players want to win. However, I think that video poker offers players something else too. It gives them an opportunity to use their skill and ingenuity to challenge the machine. They can play at their own pace, taking as much time as they want to decide what to hold and what to discard. They can analyze the hands that appear on the computer screen; the way they play each hand is up to them.

Most of the time, there is more than one way to play a video poker hand. The players can consult the payout chart and determine which option will result in the best return for their initial bet.

That's why video poker and all the many variations of the basic game are plentiful in most casinos. It's a popular game because it offers a lot of choices to the player. It's a game that requires skill and concentration, but it can also deliver a good deal of entertainment to a player who has taken the time to learn how to play it well.

In the following chapters, you will learn the basic rules of poker and the nuances of the computerized machine. A simple, sensible playing method will be introduced, and you will learn how to adapt that method to a variety of video poker games. While this conservative method isn't for everyone, it is for players who want to get the most out of their entertainment dollars.

I began this chapter with the story of the elderly couple. I'll end it by saying that the casino I was in that day was an Indian casino in Scottsdale, Arizona. When I arrived, it was very crowded, so much so that I didn't really have a choice of video poker machines. In later chapters, I will discuss how to find a good machine, but on that day it was a moot point. There were simply no choices to be made.

I was in Scottsdale visiting friends and had been driven to the casino in their car. After walking around the casino for 10 minutes, I sat down at the only available video poker machine knowing that I probably wouldn't be leaving the casino until my friends were done playing.

No, I didn't win big. The machine I was playing wasn't what I would consider a good video poker machine, but it paid enough to keep me going. None of the video poker machines in that row seemed to be paying any better, so I didn't bother moving over when the one next to me became available. That's when the elderly couple showed up and donated their $20 to the casino. I doubt they enjoyed playing the machine. I know they didn't enjoy losing the $20 so quickly.

I, on the other hand, did enjoy playing even though the machine was a bit of a dud. I put $10 into the machine and played steadily on that $10 for almost three hours. When my friends came to collect me, I cashed out my credits and pocketed six dollars in quarters. By playing conservatively, I got the most from my entertainment dollars and, unlike the elderly couple, walked out of the casino feeling like a winner.

That's the result I want for every person who reads this book. I want you to walk out of the casino feeling like a winner because you enjoyed your time there and still have money in your pocket or purse.

CHAPTER 2

Learn the Basics

Before you risk money on any gambling device, you should know the basic rules of the game you are playing. The casinos want to encourage players by making the games fun and appealing, so, for the most part, the rules are simple and easy to follow.

While my relatives delighted in making up strange rules for our family poker games, the machines don't declare one-eyed kings wild. Variations such as Deuces Wild and Joker Poker can be found, but Jacks or Better, five-card-draw, poker is the most common and popular casino offering.

The order of winning hands, beginning with the highest hand, is displayed on the payout schedule on every video poker machine. The casinos show the hand with the biggest payout first to attract players, but remember that the odds against getting a better hand rise along with the payout amounts. I have listed the winning hands in the opposite order because the lower-paying hands are the ones that come up most frequently on video poker machines.

For the benefit of those of you who have never played poker, or even looked at a deck of cards, there are 52 cards in a standard poker deck divided into four suits: hearts, diamonds, spades, and clubs. Each suit contains a two, three, four, five, six, seven, eight, nine, ten, jack, queen, king, and ace.

The winning poker hands are as follows:

One pair of jacks or better (this includes jacks, queens, kings, and aces)

Two pair (twos through tens)

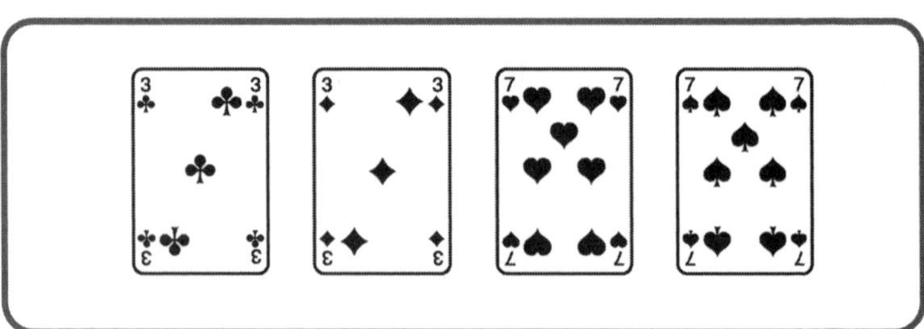

Three of a kind (three cards of the same numerical value)

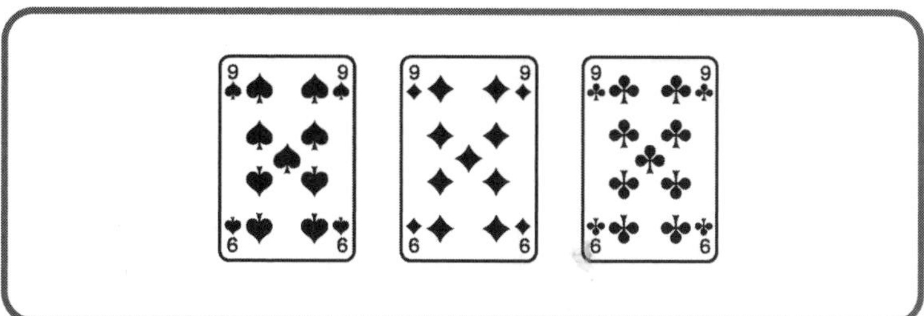

Straight (five cards in consecutive numerical order regardless of suit)

Flush (five cards in the same suit regardless of numerical value or order)

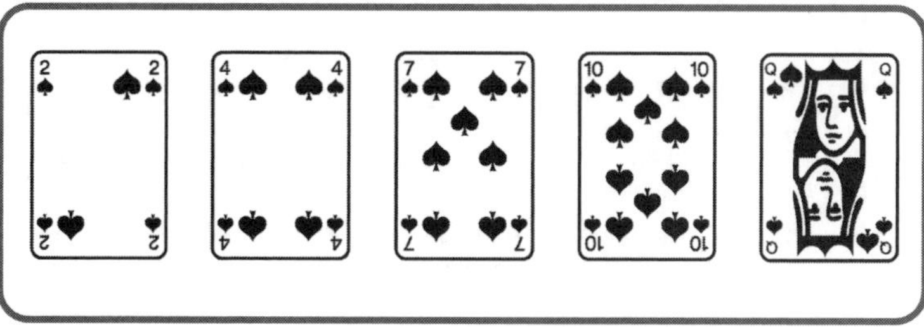

Full house (three of a kind plus one pair)

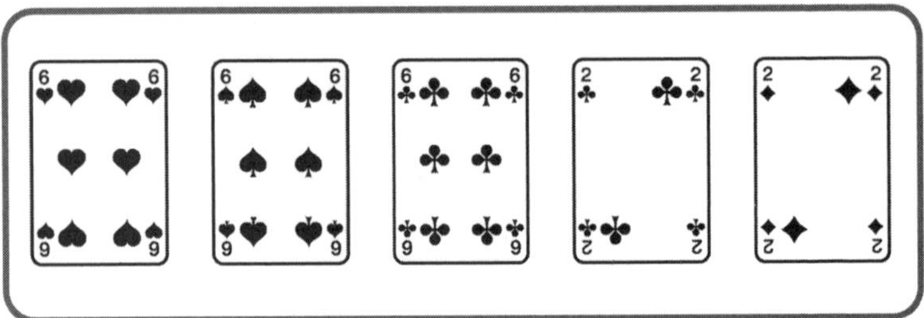

Four of a kind (four cards of the same numerical value, one from each suit)

Straight flush (five cards in consecutive numerical order in the same suit)

Royal flush (ace, king, queen, jack, and ten in the same suit)

Two values can be assigned to an ace. It can be either the highest or the lowest card in the deck. In the royal flush illustrated above, the ace is the highest card in the deck, but it can also be used in a straight or straight flush as the lowest card in the deck with a numerical value of one.

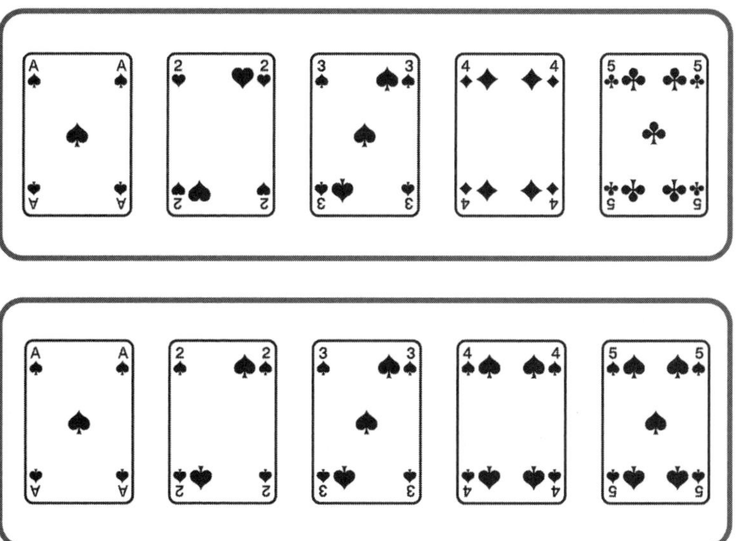

Some video poker machines pay out on a single pair of tens or better, but they are few and far between. If you encounter such a machine, your odds of winning are slightly increased. You have another chance of recovering your initial bet because an additional winning hand has been added to the payout schedule.

You should become familiar with the winning hands and their order in the payout schedules, from top to bottom or bottom to top. However, knowing the order of winning hands isn't enough. You should also become accustomed to the way the cards are dealt and learn to recognize the different ways the cards displayed on the screen can be played.

When you start dropping coins into the machine or putting your bills into the currency slot, you should do so with the confidence that you know what it takes to win and are ready to beat the machine at its own game.

CHAPTER 3

Winning Ways

Five-card draw, Jacks or Better, is the standard fare of video poker machines. Once you have mastered this game, you can move on to any of its variations.

As the name implies, the minimum you need to win a hand is a pair of jacks. A single pair of queens, kings, or aces will also satisfy the requirements of the lowest-paying hand in this game.

Before you risk real money, you should spend some time practicing the game. Part of the fun and an important step to winning consistently is the ability to recognize the potential or lack thereof in each hand dealt by the machine.

Handheld versions of video poker are inexpensive and fit in a pocket or purse. Most have a musical tone that sounds when you are dealt a winning hand. Fortunately, it can be turned off, and you can play silently anywhere. It may make those long waits in the banks, grocery stores, and doctors' offices more bearable. The one I use starts you off with 100 points and keeps track of your wins and losses. If you lose the first 100 points, the game resets itself and gives you a new set of points.

If you own a computer, you can purchase a video poker game to play at home. If you have access to the Internet, there are a number of game sites that allow you to play video poker for free. My favorite video poker games are on pogo.com and iwon.com. However, when you play on any of these free sites, you'll be bombarded with ads for on-line casinos that are not free.

Don't be tempted to try out your video poker skills at on-line casinos, which operate via credit cards. Having worked for an Internet company that processed credit cards for on-line casinos, I know how quickly those betting debts can accumulate on your credit card account. In addition, the research I did for the book I wrote on bankruptcy proved that uncontrolled credit card spending is the fastest, surest way to get into financial trouble. Gambling should always be done on a cash-only basis.

Also keep in mind that most on-line casino companies are located on obscure islands where gambling isn't regulated. Casino gaming needs to be regulated. Let's face it: the odds are already tilted in the casino's favor. How else could the casino afford to stay in business? The purpose of gaming regulations is to keep those odds from being further manipulated and stacked against the players. So, if you're playing on an Internet site, ignore those ads for virtual reality casinos and concentrate on improving your gaming skills for the video poker machines that physically exist in an actual casino where you are protected from illegal gimmicks and practices.

Now that the sermon is over, let's get back to the strategies that will allow you to play video poker with the least amount of risk.

Although I have been playing and winning at video poker for years, I still practice on my handheld game and on my favorite computer sites. A baseball player doesn't stop going to batting practice when he makes the major leagues. Batting practice helps him to recognize all the different types and speeds of pitches that sail toward the plate. Batting practice helps him to adjust his swing to a variety of pitches.

Kids in my neighborhood played baseball in the schoolyard next to my house. There weren't enough boys in the neighborhood to form two teams, so they graciously allowed girls to play. Three strikes for the boys and they were out at the plate, but we girls contended that we didn't know how to play as well and insisted that we get five strikes instead. Women's lib aside, my girlfriends and I just wanted to increase our chances of hitting the ball and winning the game.

That's what you are doing when you work on your video poker skills. You are taking batting practice, allowing yourself as many strikes as needed to become adept at winning the game.

Most video poker hands are playable in that they contain some potential for winning. A few are so bad that your chance of winning is best served by discarding all five cards and getting new ones.

To simplify the strategy, I'll be instructing you to hold the cards that have the best possibility of resulting in a winning hand. Other possibilities for a better payout may certainly exist, but the point of these examples is to provide you with a preview of the "play the favorite to show" system and to stress the way a hand should be played to give you the best chance of registering a win.

If you are dealt an automatic win, such as a pair of jacks, queens, kings, or aces, you hold the pair and discard everything else. You may improve your hand and get a higher payout, or you may not. At the least, you have a sure win and will recover your initial bet.

A single ace, king, queen, or jack or a combination thereof has potential. If you have no pairs and no decent hope of getting a straight or a flush, hold the higher cards and go for jacks or better.

Hold the jack and the ace and discard the rest. There are three other jacks in the deck and three other aces, so drawing one or the other is your best chance at jacks or better and a winning hand.

In the absence of jacks or better or a higher winning hand or a deal that contains four to a flush or a royal flush, I look for a lesser pair to hold.

If dealt the above hand, hold the eights and discard the rest. It is a lesser pair that won't garner a payout on its own, but consider the potential. Three new cards could provide another eight for three of a kind, another pair for two pair, or two more eights for four of a kind. Although the possibility is remote, you could also receive a different set of three cards of the same numerical value to produce a full house.

As a general rule, I always hold a pair regardless of its numerical value. The exceptions to this rule touched on above will be discussed in more detail in a subsequent chapter.

Holding the other winning hands on the list, such as three of a kind, straight, flush, full house, four of a kind, straight flush, and royal flush, should be obvious and automatic. The more you play, the more you will see some of these winning hands appear in the initial deal. Of these hands, three of a kind has the most potential to result in a higher winning hand of four of a kind or a full house.

Most video poker machines flash or highlight the payout when a winning hand is dealt. Some display the title of the hand over the cards. This decreases the possibility that a player will miss a winner and inadvertently discard it and lose the hand. However, to be on the safe side, take the time to look over each deal carefully. There is no time limit on holding or discarding cards, so relax and play at your own pace.

Watch for "almost wins," as shown in the following examples. An almost win is a deal that only needs one more card to make it a winner.

Discard the seven of spades and hope for another heart to complete the flush.

Discard the ten and try for an ace or six of any suit to give you a straight. This is an almost win because the straight can be completed by drawing a card that fits on either end of the numerical order of cards. With four aces and four sixes remaining in the deck, you have a fighting chance to complete a winning hand.

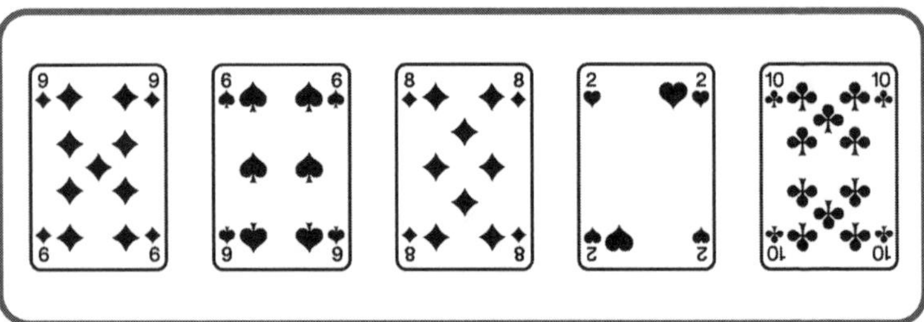

With no face cards to hold, the most sensible way to play this hand is to discard the two of hearts and go for the straight. There are four sevens in the deck, and if you're lucky you may draw one of them to replace the two you discarded. Because the card you need is in the middle of the numerical mix, you'll be trying to "fill an inside straight." Your chance of turning this deal into a winning hand is less than that of the previous example, but it can be done.

A deal that provides no sure win, no face cards, no lesser pairs, and no almost win isn't a welcome sight on the video poker screen. Sometimes they still have potential, as in the following example.

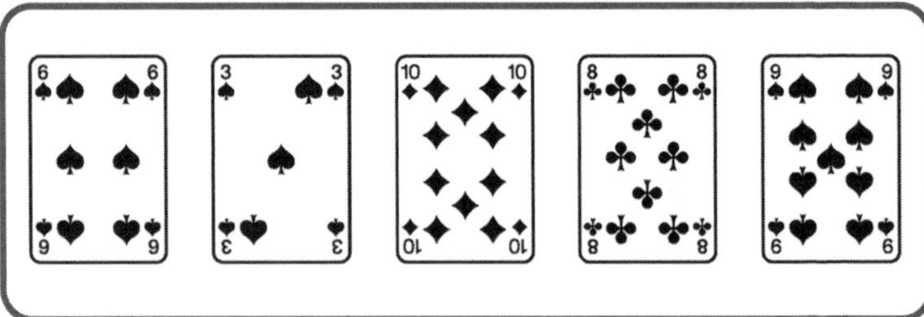

If I'm dealt a hand that has three of the same suit, that's what I hold. The probability of getting two more cards in the same suit isn't great, but it's possible. After all, there are 10 more spades in the deck.

If the deal has no sure win, no face cards or lesser pairs to hold, and no almost wins to hold, and doesn't even contain three cards of the same suit to hold, it has no potential and should be discarded. Simply push the deal button on the computer, and those five cards will be replaced by five new ones. Discarding the whole hand should be a last resort because, when you do that, you are stuck with the new hand with no chance of bettering it.

These strategies and suggestions should give you a good idea how to play Jacks or Better poker. As you practice and become more skilled at the game, you'll probably develop a few strategies and tricks of your own.

A player who sat next to me at a video poker machine in Nevada claimed that, when you are dealt three of a kind, you should wait 30 seconds before holding the three cards and going for four of a kind or a full house. He said he usually bettered his hand by doing that. I tried it several times and must report that it never worked for me. In fact, I got better results when I just held the cards and drew new cards immediately. However, I told my brother-in-law about it, and he claims that it works like a charm. Three times in a row he got four of a kind by counting slowly to 30 before drawing. Maybe I'll have to give this strategy another try.

Gamblers love to give each other tips and advice. It's part of the fun of being in a casino. It's one of the reasons I'm writing this book. I've tried a lot of things over the years — some worked, some didn't.

As long as the proposed strategy doesn't have you doing something dumb, such as discarding a winning hand, try it and see if it works for you. But remember that the best way to play is the one that brings you the most enjoyment.

For me, it's the satisfaction of playing longer on less money. I don't mind breaking even, but I hate to lose. Since I know that Lady Luck is a fleeting, elusive companion, I rely on myself, the strategies I just outlined, and the method I'm about to share with you to keep me in the game.

CHAPTER 4

A New Game Plan

If you read the introduction, you'll remember the story of Benny the Bookie and the advice he gave to me: "There's only one thing you need to know about gambling, little lady. If you're going to bet, play the favorite to show."

I don't know why his words had such an impact on me. Maybe it was because Benny was the first bookie I ever met. Maybe it was because he made me feel important by allowing me to watch his newsstand while he ran off to place bets for his customers. Maybe it was because, even at the tender age of seven, I was interested in gambling. At any rate, his advice was stored in my memory bank until I became old enough to put it to use.

As I also explained in the introduction, the first time I put Benny's advice to the test was at the racetrack. This was a logical choice since his expertise centered on horses and racetracks. Sportsman Park was located on the south side of Chicago. During the day, the park held regular races in which horses ran around the track carrying jockeys who guided them toward the finish line. At night, Sportsman Park featured harness racing: instead of being seated on the back of the horse, the jockey sat in a cart and was pulled along the track. In a harness race, the jockey controls the horse with a set of reins that extends from the cart to the horse's bridle.

I'd never actually bet on a horse race before, but one evening I went to Sportsman Park for the harness races with a group of friends. For most of us, it was just a different place to spend the evening, a new diversion. Of course, the guys in the group knew all about racing and were eager to impress the girls with their knowledge.

As one of the boys showed me the racing form and explained how to place a bet, I heard the magic word *favorite*, and Benny the Bookie and his words instantly sprang to mind. "What's the favorite?" I asked, suddenly very interested.

"The horse that is expected to win the race," my friend explained. "The bookmakers study all the horses in a race, their breeding, their trainers, their jockeys, and the other races they've run, and determine how the horses will do in that particular race. Once all the horses in the race have been evaluated, the bookmakers predict which horse has the best chance of winning, and the odds are set."

I listened intently as he went on to tell me how to place a bet on a particular horse.

"You pick the one you want and decide if the horse will win, place, or show in the race."

I soon understood that if you played a horse to win you could collect only if it crossed the finish line first. A place bet allowed you to collect if the horse came in first or second, but a show bet meant you could cash in a winning ticket if the horse came in either *first*, *second*, or *third*.

It was a short leap to realizing that a show bet actually gave the player three chances to win, and Benny's words suddenly made perfect sense. Take the horse that the experts say has the best chance of winning the race and bet it to show. That bet increased the likelihood of recovering the amount of the initial wager and realizing a profit.

When a horse finishes in one of the top three spots, it is said to have "run in the money." The racing programs provide statistics on all the horses competing in a particular race: the number of times the horse has raced in the current season and the number of times it has run in the money.

A horse not expected to run in the money can have very high odds, say 20 to 1. That means, if the horse were to win the race, anyone who placed a bet on it would receive $20 for every dollar bet. That sounds great, but those horses are called "long shots" because your chances of winning aren't good.

Since racetracks and bookies are in the business of making money, the favorite usually has low odds. The odds on each horse go up or down depending on how many people are placing bets on it. If a lot of bets are placed on a horse, its odds go down; if only a few people are placing bets on a horse, its odds go up. So, when a favorite runs in the money, the payoff on the winning tickets isn't going to provide a down payment on a snazzy sports car or even a tank of gas. What it will do is give you back your initial bet and a small profit. The real advantage is that, even though you're not winning big bucks, you're not losing money either. You can put the profit aside and take your initial betting money and play the next race.

The method was simple, and I used it on every race that first evening. There were a few upsets, times when the favorite didn't run in the money, but they were offset by the times the favorite came in third. When the horse came in third, I got a bigger payoff because, by placing a show bet, I was saying that was how I expected the horse to finish in the race.

The weekend harness races became a regular source of entertainment for my social group. Sometimes we'd go to clubs and shows and get to the track just in time for the last four or five races. We liked to do that because, when you arrived at the track after the fifth race, you didn't have to pay the admission fee. By that time of the evening, the track vendors were no longer selling racing programs, so we'd stand at the gate and ask people who were leaving the track if we could have theirs. The guys in the group weren't too successful in the art of bumming free programs, but the girls just had to smile sweetly at an exiting male to land a program.

Now I'm definitely not suggesting that you go to the racetrack, try to get in free, and beg for a program. I'm just telling you what my friends and I once did. To us, it was all part of the fun. Being at the track, mingling with the racing crowd, talking to experienced horse players, and cheering our horses on to the finish line were entertaining. I didn't go in expecting to win big; I was happy to make a small profit or just break even.

To me, it was a numbers game — and it still is. Why give yourself only one chance to win when, for the same amount of money, you can give yourself three chances to profit on your initial bet?

Over the years, I have talked to many racing enthusiasts who think I'm wasting my time and money betting on a horse to show. "Not enough profit," they tell me. "What can you do with 20¢ profit? Bet to win and get some real money."

For those of you not familiar with racetrack betting, the minimum payoff on a two-dollar bet is $2.20. Twenty cents doesn't even buy a phone call these days, but the important thing is that you get back your original bet of two dollars and can use it to bet on the next race.

If you bet the favorite to win and it comes in second or third, you get nothing. You've lost your initial bet and have to come up with another two dollars to bet on the next race. To put it bluntly, you're a loser. Winning is a lot more fun.

Horse racing — like any other form of gambling — isn't an exact science. There is always the element of surprise, always the possibility that you will double or triple your money on a bet. There are also times when the favorite doesn't run in the money. One time the favorite I'd bet on fell over dead just a few feet from the finish line.

That intangible, unpredictable aspect of gambling is what makes it exciting. When you place a bet of any kind, you are matching your wits against the odds. By tempering your desire to win with common sense and logic, you may be able to adjust those odds in your favor more often. Playing the favorite to show at the track gives you three chances to make money, and it follows that applying this simple, low-key technique to other gambling venues will increase your probability of playing longer and winning more often.

You've already learned the basics of Jacks or Better poker and reviewed strategies designed to help you determine the best way to play each hand. In the coming chapters, you'll see how other aspects of playing the favorite to show can be applied to Jacks or Better poker and a number of other video poker games.

Remember that driving a flashy sports car may be fun, but once the car runs out of gas the game is over.

CHAPTER 5

Smart Wagers

There are nickel machines, quarter machines, and dollar machines. Since this book proposes a conservative way to play video poker, dollar machines aren't recommended. However, if you are inclined to make larger bets, you can play dollar machines using the same method suggested for nickels and quarters.

The maximum bet on most nickel video poker machines is five nickels for a total of 25¢. Some nickel machines allow you to bet 10 nickels per hand, but I don't recommend playing them. If you're going to bet 50¢ on a single poker hand, you may as well move up to the quarter machines. I think they pay better.

Before you put money into any machine, look at the payout schedule posted at the top of the machine. The top payout is always a royal flush, and on a nickel machine it usually pays 4,000 coins or $200. That's an excellent return on a 25¢ bet — be aware, though, that a royal flush occurs only once in every 44,000 hands. That doesn't mean you can't walk up to a video poker machine and get a royal flush on the first deal. It can happen. It's just not very likely to happen.

I played video poker for several years before I got a royal flush. It had nothing to do with the method I was using. It had everything to do with how tough it is to draw that hand. A royal flush pays the most because it is the most difficult hand to get.

My first royal flush was on a nickel machine on a carousel of machines near the casino cashier. We'd just arrived at the casino, and my husband was at the cashier getting change. I had three nickels in my pocket and started dropping them into the machine, playing one at a time to make them last longer. This wasn't what I ordinarily do. I always bet the maximum amount on a nickel poker machine, but I wasn't playing the machine in earnest. I was just killing time while I waited for my husband. In retrospect, I wasn't playing wisely and was very lucky to have experienced a happy outcome.

Anyway, after three hands, I had five credits on the machine, and my husband was motioning for me to follow him to another part of the casino. I pushed the maximum bet button, and the computer dealt me three face cards, all diamonds. I held the diamonds thinking I could get jacks or better or a regular flush, but the computer dealt me the ace and ten of diamonds, and the machine started flashing and beeping. I'd hit my first royal flush.

I looked around for my husband, but he was gone. Strangers were passing by and congratulating me as the machine continued to flash and beep. I was stunned. The one time I wasn't playing in earnest I hit the top prize: 4,000 nickels or $200. I'd just been trying to use up the last of my credits and move on, and there it was, arriving like an unexpected gift or a surprise visit from an old friend.

The point I'm making is that it can certainly happen any time, and when it does it's great. Still, in most instances, if you play solely with the idea of getting the top payout, you'll be out of money long before that 44,000th hand comes up. Based on a bet of 25¢ per hand, you could spend $11,000 before the next royal flush appears on the computer screen.

So, when you contemplate payout schedules, pay more attention to the lesser wins. Jacks or better and two pair are dealt on a steady basis. All machines pay even money on a single pair of jacks or better. Most machines also pay even money on two pair, but some will return two times your bet on two pair. Those are the machines I try to find and play. Getting two pair is common, an easy win, and doubling my money on an easy win allows me to play longer for less.

A standard piece of advice for video poker players is to find a machine that pays eight or nine to one on a full house. Those machines are supposed to pay better overall. That may be true, but I'd rather find a machine that pays out more on two pair or three of a kind because those hands are going to come up a lot more often than a full house.

Once you've settled down at a machine and put money into it, don't think you have to stay there. I never stay at a machine that doesn't pay. There are times when a casino is so crowded that it's impossible to jump from machine to machine, like the situation I related in the first chapter. However, although the machine I played in that busy casino wasn't paying well, it was paying enough to keep me playing it. I have a minimum I expect to receive from any gaming device. If it doesn't deliver, I leave it and look for another way to amuse myself.

What's the minimum I expect from a video poker machine? It's one winning hand out of every three deals. If I play hand number four and still haven't registered a win, I cash out and go to another machine. Now it does not have to be a major win to keep me at any given machine; it just has to be enough of a win to keep me even or reasonably close to my initial investment. I keep an eye on my credits and calculate whether a good hand, such as three of a kind or a full house, will bring me back to my original credits.

I suggest that, when you are going to play nickel machines, you have a few rolls of nickels or small currency to insert into the machine. Break your big bills into coin rolls or fives and singles so that if the machine isn't paying you won't have to cash out and lug around a heavy bucket of nickels.

The trend is toward new machines that don't take coins and pay out by printing a neat cash receipt that you can either insert into another machine or take to the cashier and exchange for cash. If you're going to keep playing, don't let the cashier give you big bills for your cash receipt. Ask for smaller bills. The casinos have more cash on hand than most people will ever see in a lifetime.

While I'm on the subject of currency denominations and walking away from a machine that isn't paying, let me mention the player cards that casinos give to customers. Slot club cards can be inserted into any machine. As you play, you accumulate credits on the card, which can then be exchanged for all kinds of things. Free food, free rooms, or free merchandise can be earned with points on a casino club card. That's all well and good, but I think the casino has an ulterior motive in giving you the card and offering you the perks associated with it.

When you insert your card into a machine, it usually tells you how many coins you have to play to obtain the credits on that machine. There is a tendency to stay at a machine and keep playing it until you've satisfied the requirement and received your points. If you are winning, that's fine, keep playing and getting the points; if you are losing, though, forget the points and move to another machine.

Staying at a machine that is just taking your money and not giving you anything in return may cost you a lot more than that free dinner the casino offers in exchange for those club points. In fact, you may be able to buy yourself three dinners on the amount of money you spend trying to earn enough points to get just one free meal. Club cards are fine, but use them with discretion and on your own terms.

When you apply the play the favorite to show method to a Jacks or Better video poker machine, you concentrate on getting a winning hand. Any winning hand is good. All you are trying to do is keep enough of your own money to keep playing.

Let's look at more sample deals and discuss how they should be played using this method.

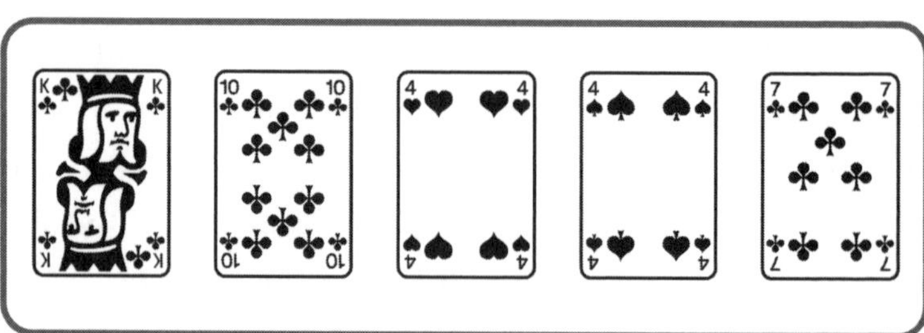

You could go for a flush since you have three cards in the same suit, but keep in mind that a flush is higher up on the payout schedule. The higher the payout, the more difficult the hand is to complete. Two pair and three of a kind are lower on the list. They don't pay as much but are easier to get, so, if you are dealt a hand like the one shown in the above sample, your best chance of a payout is to hold the fours. It's more likely that you'll draw another pair or a third four for a win than two more clubs for a flush.

In the absence of a pair or three in the same suit, hold single aces, kings, queens, or jacks to go for jacks or better. Jacks or better is not a big win, but, like a show bet at the racetrack, it keeps you even.

In the above example, you'd hold the ace, king, and queen. Another of any one of them will give you jacks or better. Also, you have three to a straight, not a good likelihood for a win but one that exists all the same. A jack and ten in any suit would give you a straight.

This hand doesn't leave you with much choice. You would, of course, hold the king of spades to try for another king and a minimum jacks or better win. I'd also hold the ten of spades, just because it would allow you to capitalize on the remote possibility of a royal flush. As a gambler, you should be an optimist as well as a realist.

Here is a hand that presents a true dilemma. Should you discard the ace and try to fill the inside straight by getting a five? Or should you discard everything but the ace and go for jacks or better? The answer lies in the number of credits you have on the video poker machine and your own instinct. If you have extra credits to risk and you are feeling lucky, go for the straight. Otherwise, take the safer route, hold the ace, and go for the lesser win of jacks or better.

Video poker machines are computers that can be programmed in a multitude of ways. There is no way to calculate the odds of getting a particular hand on any one deal, but over time I've learned that the lesser-paying hands are dealt out more frequently.

Instinct plays a large part in the success or failure of any venture. Gambling is no exception. Learn to trust yourself and make choices that feel right to you. The more you play video poker, the more adept you'll become at trusting yourself to make the right choice on any given hand.

One time another gambler seated next to me watched me go for an inside straight and was impressed when I got it. "Going for an inside straight takes guts," she said. "I never try for those."

"It depends on my mood and how many credits I have," I replied honestly.

Perhaps a more accurate statement might have been "It depends on the machine." That's because, when I'm faced with a deal like the last sample hand, my decision regarding what to hold and what to discard is usually based on how much I like the video poker machine I'm playing at the moment.

The fact is that some machines pay better than others. They are computers programmed to be generous or stingy with their payouts. The other thing you must keep in mind is that video poker machines go through cycles. They have winning cycles and losing cycles. How often have you heard people say that they won a lot of credits and then gave them all back to the same machine?

This brings up another rule I follow. *I never give the credits back to the same machine that gave them to me.* When I hit a big payout, I decide how much of the winnings I will use to keep playing. I never just cash out and walk away, because once a machine begins to pay it often keeps paying until that cycle is over.

For example, I recently hit four of a kind on a nickel video poker machine and got 250 credits. A few hands later, the machine dealt me four of a kind again, and I got another 250 credits. Once a machine gives you a generous payout, set a limit to risk from your winnings and keep playing until you hit that amount. After the second hit, I had over 600 credits on the machine, so I played the excess credits down to 600. By staying at the machine for a set number of subsequent deals, I determined that the machine's winning cycle had ended. I know that a winning cycle has ended when I begin to lose more hands than I win.

That particular session allowed me to cash out with my winnings and my initial investment of 100 credits. I started with five dollars and walked away with $30. Not a bad profit from a nickel machine.

In this example, the computer has dealt the player a pair of kings; however, it has also dealt an almost win, one card away from a royal flush or a flush. This is the one and only time I suggest throwing away the sure thing and going for the bigger win. When you hold the hearts, you are also holding three face cards, so, even if you don't get the flush or royal flush, you can still draw another face card and end up with jacks or better, the same position you started with on the deal.

The theory behind the play the favorite to show method is to go for the smaller prize, the one that has the best chance of giving you some return for your money. The best horse in the race is the one most likely to run in the money. In video poker, each hand must be played sensibly. Each hand should be analyzed to see which cards in the deal offer the best potential for a win.

Just as the favorite in a horse race sometimes fails to reach the finish line first, second, or third, some video poker hands are going to be losers. As you learned earlier, some hands are so bad that they should be discarded entirely and replaced by five new cards. However, most hands do offer some chance for a win, and some present the player with more than one winning possibility. The trick is to determine which win is more likely to occur. With the exception of an almost win with four to a flush or royal flush, a pair is like a favorite in a horse race. A pair, even a low pair, can become a winning hand much more often than three cards in the same suit can develop into a flush. It's a simple matter of numbers.

If you hold the pair of fours, you have two more fours in the deck that could be drawn; you also have 45 other cards in the mix that could be drawn as another pair. If you hold the hearts to go for the higher payout, you have a field of only 10 other cards that could be drawn to make a flush.

As you've already learned, cards in consecutive order that can become a straight by the addition of a card at either end of the sequence have more potential than a deal in which the card needed to complete the win has to fall in the middle of the sequence. Again, this is because you are doubling the number of draw cards — from four to eight — that can complete the hand.

The play the favorite to show method is easy to follow. Just look for the possibilities in each hand the computer deals and go for the one with the greatest potential to deliver a win. Practice playing as suggested in this chapter and in the Jacks or Better chapter. Speed isn't important. Take as much time as you need to study each deal before you hold and discard. You've put your hard-earned money into the video poker machine, so relax and take pleasure in the game.

CHAPTER 6

Wild-Card Games

Deuces Wild is one video poker game that does not pay out on jacks or better or two pair. There are four deuces (twos) in a standard deck, and this game operates on the premise that the possibility of drawing one or more wild cards in a hand gives the player an extra edge.

Some players play this game exclusively. I don't find it as challenging as some of the other types of video poker, but I have played it enough to know that winning requires a little different strategy.

The most common winning hand in Deuces Wild is three of a kind. Again, this is based on the possibility that a deal will contain a deuce that can be used as a wild card. For those unfamiliar with that term, it means the deuce can be substituted for any other card in the deck. For example, if the deal includes a pair of tens and a deuce, you have three tens for a winning hand of three of a kind. Also, when the deuce appears in a deal, it is usually marked "wild" or has a different graphic from the other cards in the deck.

The typical payout schedule for a Deuces Wild video poker machine bears study. The following payouts are for a nickel machine and a maximum bet of five nickels or 25¢ per hand:

Winning Hand	**Payout**
Royal flush (no deuces)	4,000 coins
Four deuces	1,000 coins
Royal flush with deuces	100 coins
Five of a kind	60 coins
Straight flush	45 coins
Four of a kind	20 coins
Full house	20 coins
Flush	15 coins
Straight	10 coins
Three of a kind	5 coins

As you can see, the lowest winning hand is three of a kind, and it returns only your initial bet. A straight returns two times the bet, a flush three times the bet, and so on up the list. A royal flush without deuces pays 4,000 coins, or $200, on a 25¢ bet. Using the play the favorite to show method, you'd still play to get the lower prizes on the payout schedule because they are the easiest wins to obtain.

Since you have to get three of a kind to get any kind of payout, there is no point in holding face cards unless the initial deal contains a pair or more of face cards. A single pair, no matter what the denomination, will not trigger a payoff. You hold the pair because you are hoping to draw an additional card of the same value or a wild card, a deuce, to use as a substitute.

One reason I don't like Deuces Wild video poker as well as Jacks or Better is that I end up discarding a lot more initial deals. If the initial deal doesn't include a pair or a deuce or an almost win, such as four to a straight, flush, or royal flush, it's usually best to discard the deal and get five new cards. On the other hand, if you do have an almost win deal, your chances of completing the win increase because of the possibility of drawing the necessary card or one of four wild cards to take its place. If you receive a deuce on the initial deal and nothing else, hold the deuce and hope to draw a pair to go along with it.

When I put money into a Deuces Wild video poker machine, I expect to get a minimum win or at least see a deuce in the first three or four hands. When a Deuces Wild machine is in a losing cycle, the deuces do a disappearing act. If you fail to get a deuce in three or four consecutive deals, it's best to cash out and go to another machine.

Another important strategy to use when playing Deuces Wild is pretty obvious, but I'll tell you about it anyway. If you receive three of a kind on an initial deal because you have two deuces to go along with one of the other single cards, hold the two deuces and discard the rest. After the draw, you'll still have three of a kind because of the two deuces along with any other card. You'll also have given yourself a chance to get the second highest win of four deuces, and I have found that it comes up a lot more frequently than a natural royal flush.

The other hands that come up regularly if the machine is in a winning cycle and dealing out wild cards on most hands are straights, four of a kind, five of a kind, and the royal flush with deuces. Be aware of the possibilities of these payouts when you are looking at your initial deal and hold and discard accordingly.

The other wild-card video poker machine is Joker Poker. This isn't as popular as Deuces Wild, maybe because a standard deck contains only two jokers, so your chances of getting a wild card to complete a winning hand are cut in half.

On my last trip to Las Vegas, I was waiting for my sister, who was lodging a complaint at the registration desk. I had time to kill and a few coins in my pocket. This time it was quarters, so I started dropping them in one at a time in a Joker Poker quarter machine. On the second deal, I got a royal flush with a joker and won 100 coins or $25. Because there are half as many wild cards, Joker Poker has a more liberal payout schedule than Deuces Wild, but the schedule of winning hands and the game itself are basically the same.

Overall, I have found that Joker Poker wins are harder to get, and I don't recommend playing these machines on a regular basis. This view is based strictly on my experience with these machines; I can't offer any statistics to support my theory. I'm sure there are gamblers who prefer Joker Poker and win regularly on these machines.

As for the unexpected win I just related, I think I just happened to walk up to the right machine at the right time. Or maybe I win while I'm waiting for other people because I'm being rewarded for my patience.

Regardless of why, how, or when it happens, it can happen to you at any time, even on a machine you'd not ordinarily play. That's one of the things that makes gambling so appealing to the masses.

CHAPTER 7

Bonus Poker Games

Bonus Poker, Double Bonus Poker, and Four of a Kind poker machines can be found in most casinos. They're not much different than Jacks or Better machines except that the payouts for a variety of four of a kind combinations are higher. They also often pay two for each coin bet on two pair. As you may recall, I make it a point to search out these machines because two pair is a consistent winner, and the play the favorite to show method is based on going for the smaller, more frequent wins.

Four of a Kind win payouts vary from machine to machine, and you should definitely read the schedules before sitting down to play a machine. I have found that machines lined up right next to each other can have entirely different schedules. So don't think that, because there is a row of like machines, they all pay the same. Read the schedules and note the differences.

There is a group of machines on a round carousel right at the front door of a Laughlin, Nevada, casino. For readers who've never heard of Laughlin, the town is 100 miles from Las Vegas just across the bridge spanning the Colorado River that separates Arizona and Nevada. It can't compare with Las Vegas or Reno in size or glitter, but it's a nice, comfortable place to gamble.

These particular video poker machines in Laughlin are all Bonus, Double Bonus, and Four of a Kind machines. I like to play them because they're in a prime spot in that casino. High-traffic areas, such as entrances in casinos, often have good-paying machines located near them. That's because many people pass by them, and, when these potential players see and hear people winning, it encourages them to start gambling.

Anyway, although all the machines in this area seem to pay pretty well, there are big differences in the amounts they pay for winning hands. The following is a comparison of the payout schedules of two video poker machines side by side on the same carousel at this Laughlin casino. These are quarter machines, and the payouts listed are for the minimum bet of one quarter.

Winning Hand	Machine 1	Machine 2
Royal flush	250 coins	250 coins
Straight flush	50 coins	50 coins
Four aces	80 coins	160 coins
Four twos, threes, fours	40 coins	80 coins
Four fives through kings	25 coins	50 coins
Full house	8 coins	9 coins
Flush	5 coins	6 coins
Straight	4 coins	4 coins
Three of a kind	3 coins	3 coins
Two pair	2 coins	1 coin
Jacks or better	1 coin	1 coin

Did you notice that the machine that pays out two for one on two pair pays out less on the four of a kind hands? While I like the idea of getting more for two pair, when I am presented with a choice between these two machines, I would choose the one that has the higher payouts for four of a kind. That's because, like many players, I have a fondness for certain hands. Although I'm delighted to get the occasional royal flush, I know that hand is not going to come along very often. Four of a kind isn't an easy hand to get either, but it seems to come up more often on Four of a Kind machines.

The standard single-deal machines have many other names and gimmicks. Acey/deucey machines pay more for four aces or four deuces. And there are machines that have big payouts for four aces with a deuce.

Some Four of a Kind machines have symbols or faces on the aces. If you get four aces and the symbols on them line up from left to right in a particular order, the payout is bigger.

Let me stress that these are still Jacks or Better machines and should be played as such. The longer you stay at the machine collecting smaller payouts, the better your chances become of collecting a bigger payout.

If you are playing a nickel machine, play the maximum of five nickels. If you are playing a quarter machine, keep in mind that you don't have to play five quarters. The big difference in payouts between five nickels and one quarter is for the royal flush. A royal flush on a nickel machine with a maximum bet of five coins pays $200. The same bet on a quarter machine, 25¢, pays $65. Whoa, you say, that's a $135 difference.

Yes, it is, and I never thought too much about it until the day I sat down at a quarter poker machine and dropped in one quarter. The machine dealt me a royal flush in lovely red hearts. I immediately started voicing my objections, complaining loudly that I got a royal flush and had only one coin in the machine.

The woman at the machine next to me said, "I'll tell

you something to make you feel better. My husband is an electronics expert, and he says that the computers are programmed to deal the top hands on smaller bets to give you the incentive to bet more the next time."

I don't know if that is true. I do know that, after working in the technology industry for several years with electronic wizards, there are endless ways in which computers can be programmed.

I suspect the woman was just trying to make me feel better. However, after my initial reaction, I realized I shouldn't have been complaining at all. I've been playing video poker for more than 30 years and in all that time have been dealt a royal flush only six times, which works out to once every five years or so. With those odds, I'm not going to change the way I play.

A roll of quarters contains 40 coins. If you play one at a time, you can play 40 hands of poker. If you play the maximum on the quarter video poker machine, you can play only eight hands on a roll of quarters. Unexpected windfalls and setbacks can happen at any time, but the longer you play, the greater the odds of winning a bigger jackpot.

Another time at the same casino on the same group of machines, I was playing one quarter at a time and accidentally hit the maximum bet button. The computer dealt me four aces and a few minutes later dealt me four deuces, and I cashed out with several hundred dollars. It just reinforces my belief that you never know when or how the more lucrative wins are going to make an appearance on that computer screen. That element of surprise makes it all the more exciting when a bigger win does come along.

Overall, I think that quarter machines pay better; whether you play the maximum or the minimum depends on your financial status. Consider this logic. If you're playing the minimum and the machine goes into a winning cycle, you can always increase your bets; if you're playing the maximum and run out of money, though, you may never reach a winning cycle.

For the most part, the payouts for a minimum bet of 25¢ on a quarter video poker machine are the same as 25¢ bet as the maximum on a nickel video poker machine. For years, I played only nickel machines, but they fill up fast when the casino is crowded, so I started studying the payouts and determined that, with the exception of the royal flush jackpot prize, one quarter bet on either kind of machine pays out about the same.

Look at the following table and judge for yourself. Both are Double Bonus Poker machines.

As this table shows, except for a royal flush, one quarter bet on a quarter video poker machine will yield the same payouts as the same amount bet on a nickel machine. So, if the casino is crowded and you can't get a nickel machine, move up to a quarter video poker machine and play it conservatively.

Winning Hand	Quarter Machine-1 Coin	Nickel Machine-5 Coins
Royal flush	250 coins ($65)	4,000 coins ($200)
Straight flush	50 coins ($12.50)	250 coins ($12.50)
Four aces	160 coins ($40)	800 coins ($40)
Four twos, threes, fours	80 coins ($20)	400 coins ($20)
Four fives through kings	50 coins ($12.50)	250 coins ($12.50)
Full house	9 coins ($2.25)	45 coins ($2.25)
Flush	6 coins ($1.50)	30 coins ($1.50)
Straight	4 coins ($1)	20 coins ($1)
Three of a kind	3 coins ($.75)	15 coins ($.75)
Jacks or better/two pair	1 coin ($.25)	5 coins ($.25)

Bear in mind that you are in control of your betting money, and it's up to you to keep yourself in check and play sensibly. The challenge of video poker should be in the game itself, not in the amount of money bet on each hand. Filling an inside straight or getting a full house should make you feel like a winner regardless of the wager.

Also remember that the money returned to you on a lower-paying winning hand is yours. If you bet one quarter and get jacks or better, you'll win one quarter. If you bet five quarters and get jacks or better, you'll win five quarters. Either way, you are just getting back your initial bet. It's just keeping you even so you can keep on playing.

I've talked to people who take organized bus trips to various casinos. "I always take a book along," some say. "That way, when I lose all my money, I can find a quiet spot and read."

"You can stay at home and read," I tell them.

Playing the favorite to show is more than a conservative gambling method. It's a way to remain in control of yourself and the games. Successful financial ventures are built with forethought and discipline.

Walking into a casino with a book in your pocket means you are expecting to lose. What fun is that? You shouldn't walk into a casino expecting to make a donation. There are many worthwhile charitable causes that could put your money to better use. If you walk into the casino with a book, it should be this one or one like it that will help you to keep your money and have a good time too.

Have a plan and put it into action with confidence and the discipline to play video poker or any other game to win.

CHAPTER 8

Multiple-Hand Games

With the introduction of multiple-play video poker machines, the games became more intricate and expensive. The game manufacturers started with Triple Play video poker games. Once these games caught on, the manufacturers and casino operators quickly saw the potential of enticing players to spend more by increasing the number of poker hands — as many as 100 — that could be played on a single machine. Of course, you don't have to play all the hands on a multiple-play machine, but most people believe that playing more hands increases their chances of winning, and they welcome the extra challenge of playing several hands at once.

These machines come in several coin choices. Most Triple Play and Five to Ten Play machines let you choose nickels, dimes, or quarters. You do so by touching one of the coin icon buttons displayed on the screen. Once you've chosen the denomination, you choose your game.

You can play Jacks or Better, Bonus Poker, Double Bonus Poker, Super Aces Bonus Poker, Deuces Wild, or whatever else the game manufacturer has installed on the multi-play machine. The display will also tell you whether the game is Triple Play, Five Play, or Ten Play. Some machines allow you to choose the type of game as well as the number of hands you want to play.

Before you decide to play any particular game, you should study the various games and their payout schedules. Touch the screen icon for the game and let it come up on the monitor. Once the game is up, you'll see icons or buttons across the bottom of the computer screen or on the machine itself with various labels.

There is usually a help icon to access instructions for a particular game. I've found that the instructions aren't always that helpful, but you already know the basics of the game, so it's okay. If you don't know how to play a particular game, select one that you do know how to play.

The computer screen also has betting icons, such as bet one and bet max, and a deal icon. Often there are corresponding buttons on the computer itself, allowing you to push the button or touch the screen icon to operate the game. There's also an icon marked pay table or see pays. Touch that icon and access the pay table for the game so you can view the winning hands and the payouts for each hand. For example, Super Aces is usually similar to a Four of a Kind video poker game with a hefty payout listed for the winning hand of four aces.

Before I choose the game, I determine which payout schedule I like the most. If you have a preference for one game, then by all means play it — but not before you check out the pay table and make sure it will deliver what you expect. If you don't have any special fondness for one game over another, play the one with the best payouts. Again, I suggest you look for the game that pays two to one for two pair.

The return to game icon will take you back to the game itself. The menu icon will take you back to the screen where all the different games the machine offers are displayed.

Once you've decided which game to play, you have to place your bet, assuming you have inserted money and your credits have been registered on the screen. Since the multi-play machines offer a choice of coin denomination, they register a dollar amount into the computer instead of converting it to credits.

Now this is where you have to be careful. If the person who played the machine before you was playing 10 hands at five coins per hand, and many of these video poker games let you play a multitude of coins per hand, the last bet stays on the machine until someone comes along and changes it. So, if you accidentally push the deal button, the computer will deduct the amount of the previous player's bet from your credits and deal the initial cards. There is no way you can change or void that bet — you will be stuck with it. Having done it myself and lost several credits, I know that you have to complete the hand before you can change the amount of the wager.

So be careful to set the bet for the number of hands you want to play and the amount you want to risk on each hand. Your wager should be determined in part by the number of hands you want to play. The more hands you are playing, the less per hand you may want to wager on each deal. Do your math and figure out how much your total bet will be before you push the deal button to start the first game. If you are playing 10 hands at a nickel a hand, you are betting a total of 50¢. If you are playing three hands at 25¢ each, your total wager amounts to 75¢ per game. Each hand you play pays out individually according to the payout schedule.

For example, if you are playing five hands at 25¢ each, you have bet a total of $1.25. When you push the deal button, only the first hand appears on the screen. The other four hands are there, but the cards are face down.

Let's assume you are playing Jacks or Better and the following example is your first hand:

You would, of course, hold the two jacks because you have been dealt a sure win. When you hold the jacks in the first hand, the same cards are turned over on the other four hands. So you have jacks or better in all five poker hands.

When you push the draw/deal button again, three new cards will be dealt to each of the five hands. You know that at the least you'll receive one coin back for each pair of jacks or better. If that's all that comes up in each of the five hands, you have recovered your initial bet. However, the real fun in playing multiple-hand poker is in the unknown. Each hand is played with its own deck of 52 cards, so you have a vast array of possibilities among those five poker hands.

Let's look at a possible scenario of the five completed hands after each has drawn three new cards.

Jacks or better win one coin.

Two pair win two coins.

Three of a kind win three coins.

Jacks or better win one coin.

Jacks or better win one coin.

This is fairly typical of multiple-hand poker games. In this example, the player bet five coins for a total of $1.25 and won eight coins or two dollars, making a profit on the hand of 75¢.

The method of play to be used on multiple-hand video poker games is the same low-key play the favorite to show system. Hold face cards, hold any pair regardless of its value in the deck, and watch for almost wins.

One benefit of multiple-play video poker is that, if you are dealt a nice winning hand, you'll get that win three, five, or ten times over. On the other hand, you are risking more on each deal and can therefore lose money on each deal.

Say you are dealt a jack and a queen on the first hand and three other low cards that don't match up. You'd hold the jack and queen and may get jacks or better in two of the five hands and nothing on the other three. Your win in that case would be two coins, which means that you have lost three coins on that game.

Keep a close watch on your credits and play for smaller, sure wins. If your credits get down too low, you can eliminate some of the hands you are playing. Take 10 hands down to five hands, three hands down to one or two. Like all other video poker machines, multiple-play machines go through winning cycles and losing cycles.

Here are a few tricks people have used successfully when playing multiple-hand video poker. If the game you are playing stops dealing you winning hands, exit that game and try one of the others. Reduce the number of hands you are playing until you build up your credits again. If you are playing quarters, switch to nickels. On most machines, this is done by touching the icon that shows the coin value you are currently playing. That action will take you back to the opening screen, where all the coin choices are shown. Touch the icon that you want to access and then go back to your game and continue playing at the lower wager amount.

If the machine you are playing doesn't allow you to change wagers that easily, you can cash out and start over. With the new machines that print out receipts, you can do this without difficulty. Print out a receipt and reinsert it into the same machine or move to another machine for a fresh start.

If you've accumulated a substantial number of credits over your initial investment, don't let any gaming device take them back again. Set a limit that you'll play your credits down to; when you reach that limit, cash out. Call me crazy, but I think the worst mistake any gambler can make is allowing a video poker machine to pay out winnings and then take them back in the same session.

The Fifty Play and One Hundred Play video poker machines can be found in most casinos now. You can bet as little as one or two cents per hand. That sounds very economical — until you realize that, if you play all 100 hands for one cent each, you are betting a dollar per game, and at two cents per hand you are wagering two dollars on every deal.

If you are going to bet that much per hand, consider playing the single-play or Triple Play quarter machines. They usually pay better. The problem with playing 100 hands is the same one I pointed out on the Five and Ten Play machines. You must keep a close watch on your credits because you can lose on every deal, unless your initial hand contains a nice-paying winner that can be held and collected on 50 or 100 times over.

When you are playing that many hands, the computer calculates all the wins and losses. For example, you are dealt and hold two face cards. Pushing the deal/draw button then automatically deals out all 100 hands. You can see each one as it is completed, but the images may be very small in order to accommodate that number of hands on the standard-size computer screen. To make up for this, the game will project a win meter on the left-hand side of the game screen that registers all your wins for that deal and tells you how much each win is worth.

The problem is, if you don't have the payout schedule for that game committed to memory, you probably won't know how much a particular hand will pay and can't make good decisions about what to hold and what to discard. Unlike single-play, Triple Play, or even Five or Ten Play poker machines, the payout schedule isn't posted on the machine or on the playing screen in front of you. To check a payout on most of the large, multi-game poker venues, you have to touch the see pays icon and leave the deal screen to verify the payout. Doing so is often necessary because the deal may have left you with more than one winning hand to complete. Knowing how much each possible win pays will help you to make an informed decision.

Although I don't choose Fifty Play and One Hundred Play machines on a regular basis, the workings of these computerized games and the ability to play so many hands at one time do hold a certain fascination for many gamblers.

In a recent session at a Fifty Play video poker machine, I was dealt four spades, an almost win flush. Here's what I got when I held the four spades and pushed the deal/draw button: the draw yielded only 13 flushes out of the 50 hands played. That means I won 26% of the hands and lost 74% of them, not a very good ratio. Although I was dealt an almost win, I lost money on the overall deal. My initial bet was 50¢, one cent per hand. A flush paid three coins for every coin bet, so I collected 39¢ for a loss of 11¢. Not a big loss, since I risked only the minimum amount of one cent per hand, but a loss all the same. If I'd been betting nickels or quarters, the amount of the loss would have been much higher.

In another brief session on a One Hundred Play video poker machine, the initial deal gave me four to a royal flush. I was optimistic as I had 100 chances to hit the jackpot and thought I would complete the royal flush in several of those 100 hands. I did get one royal flush out of the 100 and a few regular flushes, and I did receive a decent payout, but when you are betting that many hands your money is spread fairly thin. As I've mentioned, the only way you chalk up sizable credits on the big, multi-play machines is to be dealt a good winning hand that you can hold and collect on 50 or 100 times over.

Some multi-play machines have a turbo button or icon. Turbo does just what the name implies; it makes the computer go faster. The draw cards fly across the screen, completing each hand in rapid succession. But the hands are dealt out so quickly that the human eye doesn't have time to register them separately. You don't need to examine each deal as it occurs; you can monitor the deals through the win meter. Be aware, though, that speed always benefits the casino, not the player. From the casino operators' point of view, playing faster means more bets are placed in a shorter time period. This automatically increases the player's risk for bigger losses. So don't use the turbo button and give the casino and the games more of an edge.

CHAPTER 9

Jackpots and Tournaments

There is a very sleek, high-profile gaming device called an Odyssey. This machine has a variety of games. There are a few slots that are fun but nothing spectacular. It's the video poker games on the Odyssey that are fascinating to play because of the computer's cool graphics. I always tell my husband that, if I could have an Odyssey machine at home, I wouldn't have to go to the casino so often.

You won't find Odyssey machines in every casino. Perhaps they are too expensive to buy and maintain. The computer screen is taller than average, and the video poker games are dealt by a phantom dealer who wears white gloves, the dominant images on the screen.

When you place a bet, chips move from your stack at the front of the screen to the dealer's stack at the top of the screen. The white-gloved hands deal out your cards. If you don't hold and draw within a certain amount of time, the phantom dealer impatiently drums his fingers or cracks his knuckles. The dealer also shuffles the cards and tosses them from the deck with flair when you draw. If you are dealt a nice win, a full house or a flush, the dealer applauds your success.

This is the kind of video poker machine that I could sit at for hours on end. In truth, I *have* sat at Odyssey machines for hours on end. To me, it's the type of machine that gives the player his or her money's worth because it's so different from all the others. The Odyssey delivers an extra measure of entertainment along with the poker hands.

By now, you probably think I own stock in the Odyssey company, but all of this is leading up to another warning. One of the games on the Odyssey video poker menu is a Jacks or Better playoff game. When you access this game, the screen shows the playoff jackpot, which can be anywhere from 50 coins to more than 300 coins depending on how much has accumulated there.

To be eligible for the jackpot playoff, the player must bet the maximum number of coins. Most Odyssey machines take quarters, and the maximum bet is five coins. As the session progresses, the phantom dealer will periodically flip coins into the playoff jackpot to increase its total. Then, on one of the deals, the player is informed that the next deal will be the playoff game.

Now the Odyssey goes into another graphic mode, and an opponent appears on the screen and challenges the player with words and motions. Sometimes the opponent is a southern belle straight out of an old west saloon. Sometimes the opponent is a suave maverick or a river boat gambler with a tall hat and a large moustache. It's all part of the entertainment portion of the playoff.

The phantom deals out the two hands. Both the player and the computerized opponent hold and draw in a Jacks or Better game. If the player's hand wins the game, he or she gets all the credits in the jackpot. The regular game then resumes with a minimum amount to start the jackpot off again.

The Odyssey video poker venues are great fun, but, as clever and interesting as the playoff game is, the player often loses to the computerized opponent. To qualify for the playoff game, the player must bet the maximum amount each hand, automatically requiring that more gambling dollars be risked. The playoff game is nothing more than a gimmick to get the player to bet the maximum amount on each hand. It's just another type of progressive jackpot game. Progressive video poker games exist to attract players with the promise of a big win.

Most casinos have at least one bank of video poker machines around a tote board that advertises a progressive jackpot in bright lights. As gamblers play these video poker machines, the jackpot keeps increasing until someone hits a royal flush with the maximum coins bet and wins the progressive jackpot.

The play the favorite to show method isn't for high

rollers, and progressive poker games are for people who risk more to win big. However, risking more doesn't mean you'll win more. I used to risk my winnings on progressive poker games: that is, I played them when I'd won enough of the casino's money to give me a stake for progressive poker. I stopped playing progressive games when I learned some interesting facts about the games and some of the people who play them. I learned these facts from a friend's association with a professional gambler who earned a living by traveling from casino to casino winning progressive video poker jackpots.

Professional players are experts who automatically know what to hold and what to discard on every deal. That is, of course, the correct way to play video poker and the method I am proposing in this book. The difference is that these professionals are so skillful that they can play a mind-boggling number of games per minute or hour.

These players know when a progressive jackpot is ripe or ready to pay out. While I don't know the specific details, I do know that the jackpot has to have been building for a certain amount of time and has to be in the neighborhood of $2,000. Professionals don't waste their time or money playing the progressive poker games until they are reasonably sure they have a good chance of winning the jackpot. I'm told their decision to play a particular game is based mainly on the amount that has accumulated in the jackpot. It must be $2,000 or more before they move in for the big win.

Of course, anyone who sits down at a progressive poker machine can hit a royal flush and win the jackpot if it is ready to pay out. However, the skill and speed levels at which professionals play video poker are what give them an advantage over the average player. Since we know that the royal flush comes up on every machine about once in every 44,000 hands, the professional person plays at a rapid pace to make the games turn over as quickly as possible, increasing the odds that he or she will reach that winning game before anyone else does.

The play the favorite to show method in this book was designed to keep you playing longer, but to reach the playing speed of a professional gambler would take a good deal of practice. Professionals play approximately eight video poker hands per minute. You may want to try doing that. I know I did. After trying it, I learned that it isn't that easy, and for me it took all the fun and enjoyment out of the game. The key word for the people who sit at a progressive machine for hours on end, playing so deftly and quickly, is *professional.*

As an accountant, I can add up a column of figures in a flash. I don't have to think about debits and credits and where they belong in the general ledger. I know that automatically. When I first started writing professionally, typing a manuscript was a chore. Now my fingers fly over the keyboard.

You learn your trade and become an expert by working at it over time. It doesn't happen overnight. It's the same for professional gamblers. That's how they earn a living. For them, gambling is work, not a leisure activity.

Like the turbo button discussed in the previous chapter, speeding up the game gives the casino an edge. Professional gamblers know that, but they also know approximately when the jackpot is going to go, so they don't care. It's all part of their job.

The bottom line in all of this is that progressive video poker jackpots are there to entice the average person to spend more. The casinos don't care who wins the jackpot; whether you're an amateur or a professional, you still have to play the maximum number of coins in order to win it.

The jackpot grows in accordance with the amount of money deposited into the video poker machines linked to it. A portion of every dollar that goes into the machines builds the jackpot total. For that to happen without the casino losing revenue, the machines are programmed to pay out a bit less and a little less often.

Recently, I heard that the casinos have changed the odds on the progressive video poker games, making it more difficult for even the professionals to collect the jackpot. This may be nothing more than a rumor, but I believe that it's more fact than fiction.

I suggest you approach the progressive machines with caution. When the jackpot is large enough, you may be competing against professional players. You will also have to risk more on each hand, and, more importantly, the progressive poker machines don't pay out as often or as well as some of the other machines in the casino.

On the other hand, take a look at the jackpot amount; if it's $2,000 or more, the experts claim, it may be ready to pay out. If you can afford to play the maximum, give it a try. Using the play the favorite to show method will still work to your advantage by enabling you to win more consistently and remain in the game longer.

If you believe you are as quick and skilled at video poker as a professional player, you may want to enter a video poker tournament. Even if you don't feel that confident, a tournament can be a great experience.

Video poker tournaments are held on a regular basis at casinos. Some have hefty entrance fees, $500 and up, and are not for fledgling players. Others are quite reasonable and attract players of varying degrees of expertise. The entry fee covers your tournament play and some other perks, such as T-shirts, cocktail parties, and a reception/dinner for all the players.

The ones I've entered have been fairly inexpensive, with entry fees of $50 to $100. They have introduced me to an exciting new element of play. Participants are usually scheduled at random for three 15-minute sessions at machines set aside for tournament play. The machines are preset with credits and a timer. At each session, you play until you run out of credits or time, whichever occurs first. Naturally, you accumulate credits or points on the machine for a score.

Cash prizes are awarded to the participants based on the number of points they've accumulated during the three sessions. The prize range is fairly broad. Since these tournaments are promotional events for the casino, 40% of the players go home with some cash prize. Even if you don't finish in the money, the social aspects and the experience of the competition are worth the entry fee.

Although I did pretty well in the tournaments, I realized I wasn't cut out to be a professional. I played too slowly and always had credits left when the time period ended. If you have credits left at the end of the tournament session, it means you didn't play as many poker hands as you could have, and the consensus is that, the more hands you play, the more chances you give yourself to score points. However, since I ended up with good scores anyway, it showed that the way I play allowed me to win more overall regardless of the number of games played in a given time period.

That goes along with what I have been preaching regarding my low-key method of play. This system focuses on the strengths of making good choices, holding the cards that have the best potential of a win, the favorites, and discarding the cards that are long shots.

The majority of people who read this book will never

enter a poker tournament or competition. There will be no time constraints placed on them at the casino machines. Life is complicated enough, and one of the best things about following a conservative method of gambling is that it allows you to play wisely and at your own pace.

CHAPTER 10

Spin and Win

For gamblers who enjoy video poker and slot machines, there is Spin Poker. Spin Poker is an amusing and clever combination of both. It can be played in a variety of coin denominations and has the usual array of video poker games.

The similarity between this gaming apparatus and a slot machine is in the presence of three reels, each representing a deck of playing cards that spin when the draw button is touched. Part of the fun of slot machines is watching the reels spin and listening to the sounds they make as they revolve and then settle into final position. Spin Poker works the same way.

Once the reels stop spinning, the winning hands are displayed on the screen. Each of the three reels can produce a winning hand individually in a straight across horizontal display or in combination with each other in six other intricate patterns down and diagonally on the reels.

One of the things that causes me to smile when I look at the games on multiple-choice machines is the game names. It seems that each name attempts to outdo the other by increasing the bonus description. There's Bonus Poker, Double Bonus Poker, Double Double Bonus Poker, Super Bonus Aces Poker, and recently Triple Bonus Poker has been added to the mix. Most Spin Poker machines also offer Deuces Wild and the standard Jacks or Better games. When choosing a game, remember that, no matter what the name implies, you should check out the pay tables to see which game offers the best return for your bet. As you know, the "bonus" games pay out better for hands that are more difficult to obtain, such as four aces, and pay less for more ordinary wins, such as two pair.

While only three decks of cards are used in Spin Poker, one for each reel, winning hands can be realized through six other combinations of those three reels, increasing the number of hands you can play to nine. That means you can place a bet on each of the nine ways a win could be produced.

Before you begin the first deal on Spin Poker, you have the option of playing from one to nine lines and of betting from one coin to five coins per line. Like other machines reviewed in this book, the machine will retain the last player's bet, so it's important that you look carefully and make sure you're not risking more than you intended before you push the deal button. Once you have determined how many lines to play and how much you want to bet on each line, you can set your own bet.

Buttons on the front of the machine can be pushed to choose nine lines, one coin per line, which is the bet I suggest you use to get the full effect and most enjoyment from a Spin Poker game. After your bet is set, you can use a button labeled "Repeat Bet" to continue the same bet on subsequent games.

Except for the horizontal wins on the three reels, the other winning patterns are a little crazy and would be too confusing to diagram on paper. I played Spin Poker for over an hour trying to chart the wins across the wheels and ended up with a drawing that looked as congested as the California freeways at rush hour. While I'm not going to try to reproduce that drawing, I can assure you that, if you hold a pair of jacks, those cards are held on all three reels and intersect in every way the machine calculates a win. You will get at least the minimum payout for jacks or better all nine ways. Of course, you could also draw a more lucrative combination of cards and win more on some of the lines.

The initial deal shows on the middle reel of the Spin Poker machine. You touch the screen or the hold buttons on the front of the machine and then touch the spin/draw button. The cards you've held remain stationary on the screen while the reels you haven't held on the lines spin noisily, filling in the other spaces on the reels. When the reels stop spinning, the winning hands are displayed, and the computer calculates the payouts for that game.

Spin Poker has a number of little windows on the screen to help you understand the progression of the game. On the bottom left side of the screen, the amount of cash you have in the machine is displayed in dollars and cents. The number of coins bet on each deal is shown in a window right above the cash display.

When the spin is over, every win is highlighted across the reels by a different-colored line, while the title of the winning hand is flashed in another display window underneath the reels. On the bottom right-hand side of the Spin Poker screen is a win meter that registers the number of coins to be paid for each winning hand highlighted.

There's also a larger display that tells you the total the particular game is paying. For example, if you bet one coin on all nine ways and held a pair of jacks and got nothing else on your spin/draw, the display for the total game pay would say "Game Pays 9" — that is, one coin for each line or an even return of your bet.

The only way to understand the wins on a Spin Poker machine is to sit in front of the screen and watch it highlight each win. It continues to do that after each spin/draw until you push the deal button again and start a new game. There's no time limit: you could sit there for five minutes after each spin and study the win patterns.

However, memorizing the patterns will not help you to beat this game. You beat it by using the play the favorite to show system and holding the cards that provide the greatest potential for resulting in wins.

What I don't like about Spin Poker is that you are getting draws from only three decks of cards in contrast to multiple-hand machines that draw from a separate deck for each hand played. This cuts down on some of the winning possibilities. Nonetheless, if you are dealt four of a kind, and hold it on the middle reel, you'll get four of a kind all nine ways and collect on it nine times.

The spinning of the reels may make this video poker game more entertaining for some players. On the other hand, if you are playing all nine ways, consider that, for one more coin per deal, you can play a Ten Play machine and have a better chance of winning because it deals the draws for additional hands from nine other separate decks. Each hand has its own deck, leaving 48 cards to draw from after the initial deal. In Spin Poker, there are only three decks of cards for nine possible hands.

After spending some time playing Spin Poker and observing and talking to other people who play it on a regular basis, I can report that the game offering the best return for players seems to be Deuces Wild. My sister plays Spin Poker more than any other video poker game and has collected the top jackpot of four deuces many times. So, if you like Deuces Wild, and many gamblers play this poker game to the exclusion of all the other variations, try it on a Spin Poker machine.

Thinking about how Spin Poker or any of the other computerized poker games operate may not be something you want to contemplate at all. You're in the casino to have a good time, not to analyze the way each computerized game is programmed. So, if you're confused by a particular version of video poker, don't play it. Or play it slowly, risking the minimum until you understand how it works.

The video poker machine you choose to play may be just as important as the way you play it. Find a game you enjoy playing, but don't let it or the gimmicks distract you to the point where you aren't paying attention to your wins and losses. There are just too many choices on the casino floor to stay at a machine that isn't giving you decent payouts along with the fun.

CHAPTER 11

Glimpse the Future

Over the years, you'll notice that certain games come and go on the casino floor. When a new game appears in a casino, it's sometimes on a trial basis. If the game doesn't catch on or generate enough income for the casino, it's soon replaced.

Sneak Peek Poker has been around for a while; unlike some of the more common versions of video poker, though, these machines aren't plentiful. Perhaps it's because Sneak Peek Poker machines can be frustrating. Hang around one for a few minutes and you'll most likely hear the players complaining and mumbling to themselves.

I first found Sneak Peek Poker in a Laughlin, Nevada, casino. As I was playing it, one of the casino employees came up behind me and asked if I thought it gave me a better chance of winning.

"Yes," I replied.

"You're in the minority," he told me. "Most people hate it."

Sure enough, the next time I went to that casino, all the Sneak Peek machines were gone, replaced by another type of video poker game.

Because I enjoyed playing it, I looked for Sneak Peek Poker in other casinos and found that the machines haven't been completely eliminated. Like the elusive Odyssey that I love, Sneak Peek machines aren't in every casino, but they are in some, and I think they are worth playing. Try one, if only because Sneak Peek Poker works well with the low-key, conservative system presented in this book.

The name Sneak Peek is derived from the fact that this video poker machine displays the next draw card at the top right-hand corner of the screen along with the initial deal. This means that, if you are dealt four to a flush, you know in advance whether or not you are going to get the fifth card you need to complete the win.

I suspect that some people moan and groan when playing Sneak Peek Poker because they are often disappointed to find out that the next draw card isn't going to give them the win they want. In defense of this game, let me point out that, during any session of video poker, you are often dealt four to a flush or four to a straight and then don't get the card you need to complete the hand and collect a payout. That's the nature of the game — and why it's known as a game of chance. I like to know where I stand in the game. If the next card isn't going to complete the almost win I've been dealt, I can make an adjustment.

Think about it. In a regular video poker game, you don't know if the next draw card is going to fit into your hand anyway. So, if you hold four to a flush and don't get the fifth card in the same suit, you lose. However, if you know that you're not going to get the card you need, you can discard the whole hand or hold something else in its place.

When you're playing Sneak Peek Poker, the only thing you know for sure is the first draw card. You don't know what the other draw cards are going to be, so the elements of suspense and surprise are still there.

Most Sneak Peek Poker machines are quarter machines. The following is a payout chart for a typical Sneak Peek game. The amounts shown are for a minimum bet of one coin.

Winning Hand	Payout
Royal flush	250 coins
Straight flush	40 coins
Four aces	100 coins
Four twos, threes, or fours	50 coins
Four fives through kings	30 coins
Full house	8 coins
Flush	5 coins
Straight	4 coins
Three of a kind	2 coins
Two pair or jacks or better	1 coin

For some Sneak Peek machines, the minimum winning hand is kings or better rather than jacks or better. This eliminates wins on a pair of jacks or queens, but you can adjust your holds and draws accordingly.

You will notice that the payout is also a bit lower for three of a kind. Most machines pay out three coins for that win. The schedule makes up for that by paying out a bit more on four fives through kings, 30 coins as opposed to the 25 coins other games pay for that hand. If you get four twos, threes, or fours on Sneak Peek Poker, you'll win 50 coins instead of the 40 coins listed on quarter Bonus

Poker payout schedules.

The difference in payouts isn't substantial. The payouts are more on some hands and less on others, but in the long run the difference won't make or break you as long as the Sneak Peek machine you are playing is dealing you winning cards.

Since you have a slight advantage in knowing in advance what your first draw card is going to be, you can hold and draw more skillfully. Apply the play the favorite to show technique to Sneak Peek as you would to any other single-hand-deal video poker machine.

Hold any pair, high or low, even if your next draw card doesn't match it. You'll get two additional draw cards that may match what you are holding or may match one of the other draw cards to give you a two-pair win. You'll also still have the possibility of getting three of a kind or four of a kind in the draw.

If you are dealt four to a straight on one of these Sneak Peek machines, you'll know immediately if you can complete the hand or not and hold and draw accordingly. Like any other video poker machine, sometimes it just deals you a winning hand. The next draw card is shown, but, if you've been dealt an automatic win, it's irrelevant. You will hold all five cards in the initial deal and won't use the draw card at all.

You will always know whether to hold a sure win or go

for a higher-paying hand since the exceptions don't apply when you are playing Sneak Peek Poker. You can see what your next draw card is going to be. If you are dealt four to a royal flush or a straight flush, you know immediately if the draw card is going to give you the win. If not, you can go for something else.

The following example demonstrates how this works.

Unfortunately, the draw card here isn't going to provide you with a royal flush. Therefore, you'd hold the pair of aces for a sure win and discard everything else. There are two unknown draw cards to be dealt, and you could still improve the hand by getting another ace or two or by drawing more twos in addition to the one showing.

As always, remain focused on getting the lower-paying consistent wins. That way you'll still be sitting there when the machine goes into that winning mode that results in larger returns on your bets.

Sneak Peek Poker machines simply offer a new twist on the game of draw poker. In my experience, they don't pay as well as a regular Jacks or Better game, but it's one of the gimmick machines I enjoy playing. And I've had more straight flush wins on these machines than on any others. I don't know why, nor do I care. For me, it has just worked out that way.

If you are impatient or easily frustrated, Sneak Peek Poker isn't for you. I recently sat near a man who complained aloud as he played the game. He was more amusing than annoying, especially since he kept playing the machine even though it wasn't delivering the draw cards he wanted. If he was losing his money and becoming disappointed, he should have cashed out and left the machine. Maybe he was winning, and talking trash to the machine was his way of increasing his enjoyment of the game.

Another point I should make about Sneak Peek Poker is that a lot of people who sit down at these machines don't understand the concept and lose their money in a heartbeat. Again, let me emphasize that you should take the time to study any machine you have never played before and determine how it operates before you start pushing buttons and risking your money.

As I stated at the beginning of this chapter, Sneak Peek Poker isn't all that popular. That may be another reason I like it. When a casino that has these machines is really crowded, I know I can usually find an empty Sneak Peek machine to play.

CHAPTER 12

Select the Best

The primary goal of every gambler is to win. We all want to leave the casino with more money in our pockets or purses than we had when we entered and began to play. I happen to believe that breaking even is another form of winning.

When you break even in a casino, you have used its facilities and machines for your own entertainment without any cost to you. Nowadays there aren't many recreational places that are free. Even natural venues such as parks, forest preserves, and campgrounds often charge fees to use their facilities. So the growing number of casinos around the world can be a wonderful source of free or inexpensive entertainment for adults who approach gaming with common sense and the right perspective.

When you enter a new casino for the first time, don't park yourself at the first video poker machine you encounter and start putting money into it. Take yourself on a tour and check out the different types of video poker machines in the casino. In other words, spend a little time getting acquainted with the place and its entertainment offerings.

Certain areas of the casino have machines that don't pay out as well as machines in other areas. I have found that the video poker machines in nonsmoking areas of a casino don't seem to be as liberal as machines located in other areas. Let me emphasize that this is my personal opinion. I have no information to support this theory.

Players seek out the nonsmoking areas of the casino because they don't want to be exposed to secondhand smoke, a proven health risk. That reason alone may be enough to make them stay in the nonsmoking areas even if the machines there don't pay as well as others in the casino.

I'm not saying that you can't win or stay even playing in a nonsmoking area; I just think you may be able to find better-paying machines in areas not set aside for particular reasons. Besides, if the nonsmoking area is simply roped off from the rest of the casino, the secondhand smoke is going to float over there anyway.

That said, let me add that many gambling facilities now offer a separate casino — with a variety of machines and table games — for nonsmoking players. If the casino has dedicated a substantial amount of floor space to this end, its size will dictate that it have games with decent playing odds. Two casinos in Laughlin have really nice, large areas set aside for nonsmokers. And they both have good-paying video poker machines.

Other casino areas I try to avoid are those close to the gaming tables. Again, this is my own opinion, but I think that machines in those areas pay less and as a rule operate silently because the casino doesn't want to lure any player away from a Blackjack table or a Roulette wheel, where the stakes are higher and therefore the gamblers are betting more.

It may be your first time in a particular casino, but it's likely that many of the other people you see gamble there on a regular basis. This is especially true of Indian gaming casinos located within cities and counties.

Sometimes you'll see people standing two and three deep behind machines waiting for the current players to cash out and move on. Those people are usually regulars in that casino, and they know which machines pay and which ones don't. You may not want to wait for a machine, but take note of the most popular ones for future visits.

One of the casinos I frequent in my hometown has two different banks of video poker machines that are always being played. If I spot an empty seat at one of those machines, I quickly grab it since I'm one of the regulars and know this machine is going to pay better than many of the others in the casino.

Avoid sitting down at a row that has several empty

video poker machines. It's likely that these machines aren't being played because they don't pay well.

On your first visit to a casino, look for an empty seat among a bank of video poker machines being played by others. If the casino is crowded, it may not be possible to choose, and of course, if all the machines are being played, there's no way of telling which ones are best. However, when you have a choice, here are a few tips to help you find a good-paying machine.

End machines, those located at the end of the row next to a walkway or aisle, are usually set to pay out more. In an earlier chapter, I talked about a carousel of video poker machines located at the main entrance of a Laughlin casino. I believe that, because they are located in a prime spot, they pay out better in order to attract passersby. The same holds true for most end machines, although their generosity may depend on the area of the casino in which they are located.

People always claim that the machines near the restaurant pay out better. This may be true for slot machines, but I don't think it's necessarily true for video poker machines. In fact, you won't find many such machines lining the walls near casino restaurants. That's because video poker machines take more time to play, and people waiting in line for a table don't want to commit their money to a machine they will be standing in front of for only a short amount of time.

I've found that video poker machines that make a lot of noise pay out better than the silent ones. These machines are programmed to produce a fanfare or some other type of noise each time a winning hand is collected. Again, the idea is to attract attention and make people want to try their luck by putting money into neighboring machines. The problem is that, on a bank of video poker machines, only a select few may be programmed to produce high sound levels.

When all the video poker machines took coins, it was easier to find a noisy machine. All you had to do was drop in a coin, and the machine would ding a welcome to get you started. Now, with so many casinos eliminating coins and only offering machines that take currency or cash receipts from another machine, it's a little more difficult to find a loud one.

I still think it's worth the effort, especially if you have a choice of many machines. As I suggested in an early chapter, carry some small bills, preferably singles. You can put a dollar bill in and play a hand or two to see if the game makes noise. If it doesn't pay or at least make a fair amount of racket, move on and try another machine.

Once you find a noisy machine, you can settle down for a while and play it. It's one more little trick the casinos use to attract players, and being cognizant of these subtle attention grabbers will help you to choose a friendlier, more generous machine.

As you have surmised by now, part of the play the favorite to show system entails seeking out the video poker machines that offer the most rewards to the player. The first time you visit a particular casino, it will take a little time to find the good machines, but once you've identified them you can go back to them time and again and be assured of better odds. Each machine has a number on it. If you go to the same casino on a regular basis, write down the number or commit it to memory so that you can find the machine again the next time you want to play it. Casinos are always rearranging machines, so knowing the numbers of the good machines will help you to locate them again and again.

One of the other video poker machines I look for when I go into a casino is the Double Down Poker game. It's usually a Jacks or Better game. However, the gimmick of this machine is that, whenever you collect a win, the machine takes you to another screen, where it challenges you to double your win by playing a game of High Card Draw with it.

High Card Draw is simple enough. The computer draws a card and displays it on the screen. Then it deals out a single card to the player. If the player's card is higher than the one the computer has showing on its screen, the player wins double the amount of his or her original win. If not, the original win is lost totally.

When you are playing a Double Down machine and get a winning hand on the Jacks or Better game, the computer holds the credits you have just won while a message appears. Most screens just flash the words "Double Down?" with yes and no icons. If you choose yes, you play the high-card game; if you choose no, the credits you have won on the Jacks or Better hand are added to your accumulated total.

Double Down Poker machines have also diminished in popularity. I haven't seen any new models of this game, but some of the older machines are still around. You should only play Double Down Poker if you have the discipline to say no to High Card Draw.

Double Down is a Jacks or Better game that allows you to win more frequently and consistently on the regular poker game. The concept behind it is that the game pays more often on Jacks or Better because, every time you win, you'll be tempted to play High Card Draw for a chance to increase your win.

In my experience, playing the high-card game usually results in a loss. However, if you can resist the temptation and just collect your winning credits, you can realize a profit playing this video poker machine.

Other versions of video poker take the player to another game when certain winning hands are drawn. They are fun to play because you win more initially, and they are even more fun to play if you can retain those winnings.

Some gamblers lose large amounts of money because they get greedy. They think that the $10 they just won can be increased to $20 or that the $100 can be doubled to $200. Occasionally, they do just that, but more often they lose their winnings and end up with nothing.

Casino operators count on the greed factor. They know that human nature is always tempting us to want more than we've got. Double Down machines let players win more initially because the casinos and the machine manufacturers are banking on our natural greed to make us risk our winnings on a chance to win more.

"Quit while you're ahead" is an old saying, and it's one of the most important clichés a sensible gambler can adopt. If you win it, keep it. Don't give it back.

CHAPTER 13

A Conservative Game

Another video poker game that is perfect for the conservative gambler and for the play the favorite to show system is Let It Ride.

To begin with, it allows you an additional winning hand because you can usually collect on tens or better. Let It Ride is also a table game, but, as with most table games, the stakes are set higher. Therefore, I suggest that you play Let It Ride on a video poker machine.

This game can be found on the multi-game quarter machines in most casinos. These machines offer a variety of games, including Keno, slots, regular poker, and Let It Ride.

As usual, you should check the payout table before you start placing bets and playing the game. On a typical quarter Let It Ride game, the payout schedule will look similar to the following:

Winning Hand	Payout Per Coins Bet
Royal flush	2,000 to1
Straight flush	200 to1
Four of a kind	50 to1
Full house	11 to1
Flush	8 to1
Straight	5 to1
Three of a kind	3 to1
Two pair	2 to1
Tens or better	1 to1

Notice that the payouts for a full house, a flush, and a straight are higher than the payouts on most video poker games. This is because Let It Ride is basically a five-card stud poker game. That means that five cards are dealt to the player, and the player does not hold, discard, or draw. The game is won or lost based on the initial cards dealt. Without the benefit of discarding cards from the initial deal and replacing them with new cards, it's harder to get some of the higher-paying hands. To compensate for the greater degree of difficulty, the payouts for these hands in this game are higher. The payout schedule also shows that two pair pay double the amount bet, and as you know that's always a good thing for the player.

To begin the game, you must place three bets of equal value. If you are playing on a quarter machine, you'd place three separate 25¢ bets for a total bet of 75¢.

Now, after all my advice about playing conservatively and risking minimum amounts of money, you may be thinking I've suddenly lost my focus. I assure you, though, that once you understand how this game works you'll see I'm still selling the same story.

After the three bets are in place, the machine displays an initial deal of five cards; however, only the first three cards will be face up. The other two cards on the screen remain facedown. The first of the three quarters bet is always won or lost. That first bet can't be taken back, but the other two can be. Here is the crux of the game and the element that earns it the name Let It Ride.

After examining the three cards that are showing, you decide if you want to cancel the second bet or "let it ride." Either way, once you've decided, the fourth card is displayed. Again you have a decision to make. The third bet can be canceled or taken back, or you can decide to let this bet ride. The fifth and last card is then displayed; if the five cards have produced a winning hand, the payout is made based on the number of coins that remain in the bet.

To make this more understandable, let's go through the game step by step, based on the following sample deal:

In the above deal, all the cards are of different suits, and there is no sequential order, so many winning hands are automatically eliminated. There is no conceivable way to get a straight, flush, full house, or four of a kind. However, all is not lost. The player has two picture cards that could turn into a possible win of tens or better and the slim chance that the two hidden cards could result in three of a kind or two pair.

Since we are using the play the favorite to show system, the proper decision regarding the second bet is to cancel it. Doing so reduces the risk and turns over the fourth card in the deal.

The fourth card yields a definite win in a pair of jacks. So the last decision is easy and obvious. The player lets the third bet ride. Now assured of at least an even return on the money bet, the player has the fifth and last card displayed.

The last card results in an even better win of two pair. The payout schedule shows that two pair pays out two coins for each coin bet. Since the player in this example has ended up with two coins bet, he or she will receive four coins on the payout.

On a computerized Let It Ride game, icons on the screen allow you to cancel a bet or let it ride. Although the computer prompts may vary from machine to machine, I've found that overall the displays are fairly clear and understandable, so there's not much chance of making an error.

Now let's move on to a second sample deal in the same game.

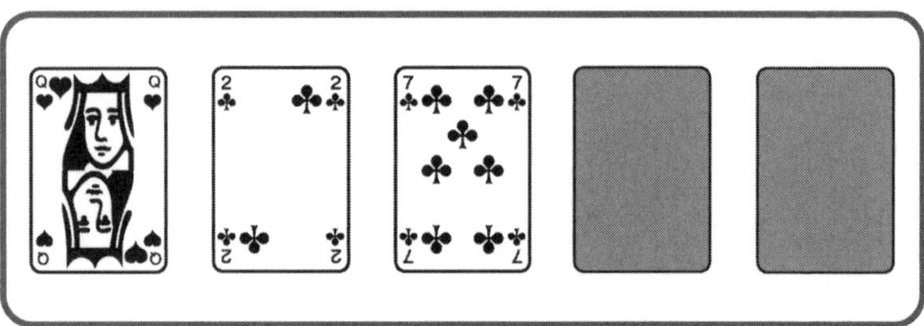

In reviewing this initial deal, you can see that you have two cards in the same suit, but the queen in another suit eliminates the possibility of getting a flush, and a straight is impossible. The best chance for a win is for one of the hidden cards to be another queen. Two pair is a possibility, though a remote one.

In this case, the player should cancel the second bet.

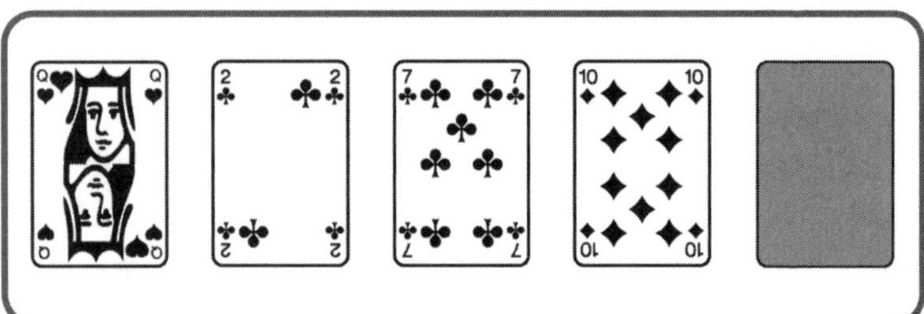

The fourth card opens up another possibility. Now, if the fifth card is either a queen or a ten, the hand can be turned into a win. Remember that the first coin is already committed to the hand. So, if the last card is a queen or a ten, the player won't lose anything. If the last card isn't one of those cards, the player will lose 25¢. However, if the player lets the third and final coin bet ride, and the last card isn't a queen or a ten, he or she will lose 50¢ or double that amount.

Based on the play the favorite to show method, the third bet should be drawn back or canceled. This is the conservative and sensible way to play this hand. It's especially prudent since, even if the last card is a queen or ten, you'd win back only your total bet or two coins. It's not possible to get anything higher than a single pair of tens or better.

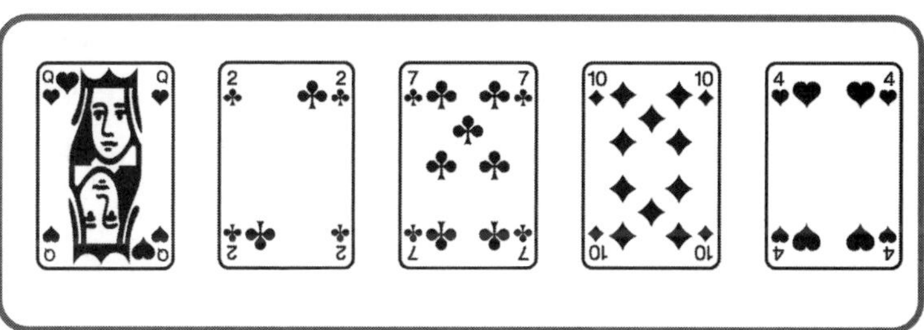

The hand is a bust, no winner, but the player who has played sensibly will lose only one coin. Since the preceding game yielded a profit of two coins, the player is still ahead of the game.

There will be times when playing Let It Ride that the

first three cards contain a pair of tens or better. Just like any other video poker game, Let It Ride deals out lesser wins on a regular basis. All video poker games do so to keep the player at the machine and encourage him or her to bet more. The smart gambler is aware of this and continues to play at a pace and a risk level that are personally comfortable.

Let It Ride is just another variation of poker, but it presents a different test of a player's ingenuity. The strategy suggested for playing it is even more conservative than the one you've learned for other video poker games.

The initial bet is three coins. The first one is always at risk, so the smart way to play Let It Ride is to draw back or cancel the second bet if you don't have at least a pair of tens in the first three cards. In other words, if you don't have a win, don't risk the second coin. Once the fourth card is displayed, if you still don't have a win, cancel the third coin bet. Doing so keeps your risk to a minimum, and, if the addition of the fifth card doesn't yield a winning hand, you've lost only one coin. If the final card does result in a winning hand, you can still collect on one of your bets.

The exception to this strategy occurs when your first three cards are all in the same suit or in sequential numerical order. In those instances, when the hand could develop into a flush, straight, straight flush, or even royal flush, by all means let your second coin ride. You'll know as soon as the fourth card is displayed whether the possibility of the bigger win still exists, and you can cancel or keep the third and final bet accordingly.

Clearly, Let It Ride requires a little more concentration and resourcefulness. They're what add to its entertainment value. As I've said over and over, gambling should be viewed as entertainment, so any game that increases your enjoyment is worth playing.

Let It Ride isn't standard fare on all multi-game machines, and, in some casinos where Let It Ride is evolving as a popular table game, it isn't on the machines at all.

As a table game, it's played the same way. You play for yourself, not against the other players or even against the dealer. Each player is dealt three cards, and then two community cards are dealt facedown in front of the dealer. These two community cards are considered part of each player's hand, yielding a five-card stud poker hand. Players look at their three cards and either ask for their second bet back or let it ride. One of the community cards is turned over, and the players ask for their third bet back or let it ride depending on how their individual hands are shaping up. The final community card is then turned up, completing all the hands, and the dealer pays all winning hands according to the payout schedule.

The big difference between playing Let It Ride on a machine and on a table is the risk involved. The Let It Ride tables I've seen are five-dollar ones. That means you buy five-dollar chips and must bet three chips per hand for a total of $15.

Although I wouldn't ordinarily risk that much, I liked the computerized game so much that I've tried my luck at the table game and, by adopting the same system, have done fairly well.

The first time I played Let It Ride at a table I was with my friend, Jane. It was during the day, and the table games weren't being played much. We sat at a Let It Ride table at the Flamingo Hilton in Laughlin. Not being well versed in playing this game at a table with a live dealer, we made the poor man a nervous wreck.

It started when we tried to slide money across the table to buy chips. He insisted the currency not be touched by human hands for 10 seconds before he picked it up and put it in the money chute. Either the dealer was new on the job or he was just very aware of the security cameras monitoring us. He was so nervous that he made us nervous.

He didn't want us to talk. He wanted us to make hand signals only, indicating whether we were withdrawing a bet or letting it ride. Jane and I are like most women. If you tell us not to talk, we talk all the more.

Let me emphasize that the dealer wasn't rude to us and that we weren't intentionally trying to upset him. He was a young man, built like a linebacker. Perhaps his size made his lack of self-confidence more noticeable to us. Perhaps he'd been pressed into service at the Let It Ride table for the first time and was jittery because he didn't think he had enough experience with the game. Whatever the reasons, the more nervous he got, the more amused Jane and I became. Then we got the giggles over the absurdity of the whole situation, and that made the dealer even more suspicious of us.

Somehow we all survived about six hands. I walked away $10 ahead, won fair and square by playing the table game exactly the way I play Let It Ride on machines.

If you've never played Let It Ride before, find it on a video poker machine and play it there for quarters before you try your luck at a five-dollar or even a one-dollar table.

CHAPTER 14

A New Game in Town

Every day manufacturers are coming out with more advanced video poker machines and new versions of the basic game. There's no way I can cover all of these in the pages of this book. The other factor to be considered in discussing particular games is that some make only brief appearances in casinos.

A few years back, I found a video poker game called "E" at the Edgewater casino in Laughlin. I don't know if the E machines were designed exclusively for that casino or not. The screen display was a clever framework in the shape of the letter E. As the cards were dealt, you clicked them into place on the framework, forming four different poker hands with cards that intersected and became part of more than one hand. The cards were dealt until all four hands were completed. Once you placed a card in the framework, you couldn't move it to another part of the E. The idea was to try to form as many winning hands as possible within the structure. I won't go into great detail explaining this game because it was short lived.

Jane and I were together again, and we got totally hooked on the E machines. We played them for hours on end. Our husbands didn't like them, and apparently they weren't alone; the next time we went to that casino, the E machines were gone. In fact, that was the only time I saw an E machine.

With that in mind, I'm now going to tell you about the latest video poker machine I discovered. This game isn't as complicated as the E machine, so I think its future is more secure.

The game is called Multi-Strike Poker, and there were just four machines on the casino floor. However, those four machines were constantly busy, another reason I believe Multi-Strike Poker will have staying power. I have a theory about new computerized gaming venues. I have no proof that this is true, but it seems that some new gaming devices pay better when they are first introduced on the casino floor. After they've been around for a time, the frequency of wins seems to diminish.

It could be that new games are played more, thus keeping the cash levels in the machines higher so they pay out more. Or it could be that, as additional machines are ordered from the manufacturers, they are programmed differently. When you are dealing with a computerized game, it can be programmed in a number of different ways.

Anyway, the four Multi-Strike Poker machines were newly acquired and paying out on a regular basis. Like most of the newer video poker machines, Multi-Strike offers a variety of games, such as Jacks or Better, Bonus Poker, Aces Poker, Deuces Wild, and so on. There's also a choice of coin denominations — nickels, dimes, or quarters. The initial bet covers four hands, so if a player chooses to bet dimes, one coin per hand, the bet on each deal would be a total of 40¢. Multi-Strike Poker allows you to play up to five coins per hand, but especially while you're learning one coin per hand is a safe bet.

Regardless of the game or the coin denomination, Multi-Strike is played one hand at a time in a progressive order. Each hand is dealt out as an individual game. A win on hand number one allows you to play hand number two, a win on the second hand allows you to move on to the third hand, and a win on hand three moves you on to the fourth and final hand.

As players successfully move from hand to hand, the payouts increase. A win on the first hand pays one time the payout schedule. Hand number two pays two times the payout schedule. Hand number three pays four times the payout schedule. Finally, if you play hand number four and win, your payout will be eight times the amount on the payout schedule. The challenge of the game is that the player must win each hand in order to move on to the next higher-paying hand.

If you lose on the first hand, you've lost your initial bet and must start all over again with a new bet and a new deal for hand one. The payout schedule for a win on the first hand is as follows:

Winning Hand	Payout Per Number of Coins Bet
Royal flush	250 to 1
Straight flush	50 to 1
Four aces	160 to 1
Four twos, threes, or fours	80 to 1
Four fives through kings	50 to 1
Full house	10 to 1
Flush	7 to 1
Straight	5 to 1
Three of a kind	3 to 1
Two pair	1 to 1
Jacks or better	1 to 1

Although none of the payout schedules on the Multi-Strike Poker machine pays two coins for each one wagered on a win of two pair, the payouts for a full house and a flush are higher than most payout schedules.

Also with this game, your goal is to keep moving up to

the next hand, which gives you the possibility of collecting two, four, or even eight times the standard payout.

A typical winning game on Multi-Strike will yield the following payouts when the bet is one coin per hand. For demonstration purposes, assume you are playing dimes, one per hand for a total initial bet of 40¢.

Hand number one = jacks or better = 1 coin = 10¢

Hand number two = jacks or better = 2 coins = 20¢

Hand number three = jacks or better = 4 coins = 40¢

Hand number four = jacks or better = 8 coins = 80¢

Total coins collected = 15 coins= $1.50

A minimum win of jacks or better on all four hands yields a profit of $1.10 on a 40¢ bet. Of course, you could lose on the first hand and lose your 40¢, but you could also register higher wins and collect a bundle on this game. If you hit four aces on hand number four, you'd collect 1,280 coins or $128 on a 40¢ wager.

Another entertaining component of Multi-Strike Poker is that it often deals out free-ride cards. These cards allow you to automatically move on to the next level even if you don't register a win on the hand you are currently playing.

Take it from a conservative player: Multi-Strike Poker is worth the extra monetary risk. Most sessions I started with $10 and cashed out with $60 to $150. The amounts I won on the Multi-Strike were what kept me coming back to play the game again and again.

Over the course of three days, I played each one of the four Multi-Strike machines and found that one of them seemed to pay better than the rest. So, of course, I made a special effort to get that machine, and, after trying all the games it offered, I determined that one of the games, Super Aces, paid out more consistently than the others.

As people came and went from the machine next to the one I favored, I learned that the game that paid out the best on that machine was Deuces Wild. I believe this is pretty common with video poker machines. Certain games pay out better on some machines than they do on others. Whether you're moving from machine to machine or game to game on one machine, it's to your advantage to try to determine the best ones to play in terms of satisfaction and profit.

Playing 10¢ a hand, I risked 40¢ on every game and found the play the favorite to show system worked well. The main strategy for Multi-Strike Poker is simple. Take any win you can get in order to move on to the next higher-paying hand.

To see what I mean, take a look at the following example:

This hand contains a win of jacks or better, but it also contains an almost win of four to a flush. If you were playing a different type of game, you might want to discard the jack of spades and try for another heart to complete the flush. This would be an especially good strategy if you were playing a multiple-hand machine, since chances are you'd get the flush on one of the hands you were playing. However, on the Multi-Strike game, you'd hold the jacks and discard the rest, ensuring at least a minimum win so that you could play the next hand.

The Multi-Strike game provides another new twist on the standard video poker Jacks or Better game. Overall, the concept of the game is easy to grasp, and, based on the fact that the new machines were constantly being played, I think Multi-Strike will soon be a permanent fixture on most casino floors. Playing Multi-Strike Poker is like climbing a ladder. The higher you go, the larger the potential payouts.

Some casinos change their machines on a regular basis, and some keep the same old machines forever. Whether you play in one casino all the time or travel around to many different casinos, you'll find that certain machines give you more enjoyment than others. Follow your instincts and play the video poker machines you like the best, but keep an open mind and try new ones now and then.

I didn't think any video poker machine would entertain me as much as the sleek, graphic-rich Odyssey, but the Multi-Strike may just push the Odyssey into second place on my list of favorites.

CHAPTER 15

Gambling Budgets

No matter which video poker games you favor, or how much you enjoy playing them, you should be wise enough to establish some rules to follow.

When the lottery was first introduced in my state, many stories circulated about people who were spending their last dollars on lottery tickets. One story told of an elderly woman who spent all her grocery money on losing scratcher tickets and went hungry for the rest of the month. I'm sure that some of these stories were true. I'm equally sure that some of them were conjured up by individuals and groups opposed to the lottery.

The veracity of the stories aside, the fact remains that all gambling presents a certain amount of risk, which is part of the thrill of gambling. For some people, gambling is addictive. Once they start to gamble, it spirals out of control, and they can't stop. To them, losing only means they must bet more on the next game to recoup those losses.

The advice in this book won't help people whose gambling habits are out of control. It's not for the high roller who risks hundreds of dollars on one roll of the dice or one revolution on the Roulette wheel. The best advice I can give to people whose lifestyles and finances are in jeopardy because of gambling is to call their local chapter of Gamblers Anonymous to get the help this organization is equipped to give.

For those who don't need to call Gamblers Anonymous, and I sincerely hope that's everyone who is reading this book, let's talk about your money and how much of it should be allocated to gaming. A gambling budget is a good idea for everyone regardless of his or her financial status.

You should have a good idea of how much money you need to meet your needs each week or month. If you don't know the exact status of your finances, sit down with a pen, paper, and calculator and figure it out. List all your income and then subtract all your current expenses. Be sure to include a fair amount for those unexpected bills that seem to crop up more often than not.

If your income does not exceed your expenses, or if you don't have a savings account to fall back on in times of trouble, the amount allotted to a gambling budget should be a big fat zero. If you do have excess funds for casino gaming, give some serious thought to the number of trips you want to make and how long each trip will last.

Indian casinos and river boat gambling have brought gaming establishments within driving distance of most people's homes. There are casinos spread all over the world, and in local communities organized bus trips are often an inexpensive and pleasant way to visit the various casinos. The cost of some of these day trips includes lunch or dinner.

Your gambling budget should include the cost of transportation and meals as well as the amount you are going to risk on the video poker machines. If you're traveling to tourist areas, you may want to add in the cost of sightseeing and shows. The amount you actually allocate to gambling should be over and above all the other expenses, especially if you are traveling to another city or country.

If your visits to the casino aren't restricted by distance or time, budgeting gambling funds is simplified. Decide how much you can afford to risk and take that amount to your local casino. As long as you are in control of the transportation, you can stay as long as you like or as long as your gambling money lasts. By using the gaming techniques suggested in this book, you should be able to stay and play for extended periods of time.

Have you noticed that all casinos have cash machines? Of course they do. The casinos want to make access to additional gambling funds as easy as possible for you. Don't be tempted to stretch your budget by using the cash machines. If necessary, leave your ATM cards and credit cards locked up at home.

Gambling should always be a strictly regulated cash endeavor. If you can't win enough to keep playing, go home and try again another day. The play the favorite to show system will keep you playing longer, but it can't guarantee that you'll win every time, nor can it guarantee that you will break even every time. No matter how skilled or conservative you become, there will be times when you may lose your gambling money. If you are playing sensibly and conservatively, those times will be infrequent, but they will still occur. That's why you need to establish a budget and stick to it. This is especially important for people on fixed incomes because, for the most part, they won't have an opportunity to recoup gambling losses by earning extra income.

Winning and losing streaks are part of the gambling mystique. Just like life in general, gambling has its ups and downs. When your best efforts to stay in the game fail, accept the fact that your luck has momentarily deserted you and stop playing. Sometimes luck and skill have nothing to do with losing. In a crowded casino, all the good-paying video poker machines may be in use by other players, leaving only the worst-paying machines available. Remember that computerized gaming devices can be programmed to pay out a lot, a little, or nothing at all.

If you find yourself in a losing cycle and aren't able to leave the casino, find a place in it where your risk is reduced or eliminated. Keno parlors and off-track betting areas present diversions from the video poker machines that allow you to sit down and relax. If you have money left from your gambling budget, you can bet on a race or buy a Keno ticket. If you are out of money, you can still watch the races on the closed-circuit television screens that broadcast the events from the racetracks, or you can study the numerical patterns on the Keno boards and talk to the players. You can stay there as long as you like without placing a wager. No one cares. Sometimes all you need is a short break. Luck is unpredictable and can change from minute to minute.

On one of my frequent gambling excursions, I failed to find a video poker machine that paid decently and decided to move over to the slot machines. I walked up to one of those machines that had a "spin till you win" symbol on the reels. I got the symbol, and the reels started spinning. I swear I stood there for so long waiting for the machine to hit a winning combination that I thought it was malfunctioning.

"That's the way my luck is going today," I mumbled to myself. "Can't even collect on a sure thing."

The machine finally stopped on a winner, and quarters started pouring out of the slot machine. I'd hit a minor jackpot. My losing streak had suddenly ended, and a new winning streak had just as suddenly begun.

Establish a gambling budget and then stick to it. Your gaming budget can be per day, per month, or per year. It's up to you and your financial condition. The important factor in setting limits for yourself is that doing so keeps you in control and focused. It helps you to play sensibly.

When you win, the excess cash can be added to your budget or put aside for other amusements. Exercising discipline over yourself and your gaming funds can only add to your enjoyment of video poker or any other gambling venue.

CHAPTER 16

Great Gambling Destinations

In recent years, the Las Vegas strip has undergone enormous changes. Many of the hotels and casinos there have become mini theme parks.

The Venetian has canals and singing gondoliers that create the illusion of being in Venice, Italy. There are foot bridges and exclusive shops, but the most amazing thing is the sky above the canals. When you enter the area, you look up and see a sky with the last light of day turning to dusk. The illusion is further enhanced by the soft floating clouds that look as real and tangible as the people gazing up at them in awe. The effect is mesmerizing, especially when you stop and realize that you entered the Venetian at 10 p.m., when it was dark outside.

At the Bellagio, dazzling fountains send huge sprays of water into the air, and the flower gardens are breathtaking. There's also a professional art exhibit. The last time I visited, actor Steve Martin had his priceless art collection on display there.

Walking through the MGM Grand hotel takes you through the rain forests and down the Yellow Brick Road. There are birds and music and encounters with waxed images of movie stars dressed for their famous roles.

In surrounding hotels, you can visit Treasure Island, Bourbon Street, or the Eiffel Tower, but perhaps the most realistic replica is the Statue of Liberty that stands in front of the New York, New York Hotel and Casino. Inside the casino, you can visit the Broadway theater district or Greenwich Village while a roller coaster filled with screaming occupants careens overhead.

All of these fabulous sites and attractions have been developed in an effort to give Las Vegas a new image as a family vacation place, and it seems that each new venue tries to outdo all the others. If you've never visited Las Vegas or haven't been there for a few years, take a trip and soak up all the sights. It's the perfect solution for a family with gamblers and non-gamblers since it fulfills the expectations of all age groups and interests.

No, I do not work for the Las Vegas Chamber of Commerce. I'm just sharing information on a place I love to visit with readers who may not have seen it for themselves. I'm also thinking that people who like to gamble may be related to people who don't like to gamble and may be able to use some of this information to talk the non-gamblers into going to Las Vegas on vacation.

Unlike some of the other spectacular gambling sites around the world, Las Vegas now caters to families. The games are exciting, and the pace can seem hectic just from the number of people who gather there on a daily basis. However, dressing up is optional, and, when the Las Vegas strip becomes too congested, there are many other casinos in outlying areas that can be visited.

Aside from the wonderful spectacles, what I like best about Las Vegas is the sheer magnitude of all those casinos lining the streets. The choices are endless, so you should never have to search too long for a good video poker machine. There are so many to choose from that finding a good-paying one is fairly simple.

Unfortunately, there is only one Las Vegas, and most of us don't get to gamble there on a regular basis. We gamble in smaller casinos and therefore must become more aware of what these smaller casinos have to offer.

When your choices are limited, you must choose more carefully and wisely. You've already read about a variety of video poker machines, and I've expressed my opinions on which are the best ones to play and why. You know that I believe the noisier the machine the more often it pays out. As for machines along aisles and busy walkways, everyone thinks they pay better. That's why the ones in the middle are often empty.

There's one more factor that should figure into the task of choosing a good-paying video poker machine: your own feelings or intuitions. If you enjoy playing certain machines more than others, you'll look for one of those machines. Why? Because your feelings based on past experience direct you to play that particular video poker game.

If you are visiting a casino for the first time, though, or are in a casino that doesn't have that type of video poker machine, you may need to make another choice. If you can find an end machine that makes lots of noise, by all means sit down and play it. If those machines are all taken, you must look at your remaining choices and rely on your psychic powers to guide you.

You may not think you have psychic powers, but you do. They are also known as instincts, intuitions, hunches, and gut feelings. Everyone has them, and they have been discussed in previous chapters. It doesn't matter whether you are in the grocery store choosing a box of cereal, at a machine contemplating the possibility of filling an inside straight, or in a new casino looking for a video poker machine to play. Trust your instincts to lead you in the right direction. It's like taking a multiple-choice test. One of the answers always jumps out at you, and that first guess is usually the correct choice. Take a deep breath and look at the available video poker machines. Your instincts will kick right in, and you'll know which one you want to try.

Years ago I was in a casino with my mother, who loved to play slot machines. I walked up to the row of slots where Mom was playing, and my instincts told me I wanted to drop some coins into a particular machine. As I raised my hand to do so, my mother reached out and grabbed my arm.

"No," she said. "Play this one." She yanked on my arm and pulled me over to the machine next to hers.

Being a dutiful daughter, I dropped my coins into the machine Mom wanted me to play. A man walked up to the machine I'd been instinctively drawn to, dropped in some coins, and pulled the lever. Bells rang, and lights flashed. The man turned to me with a puzzled look.

"What happened?" he asked. Apparently, this was the first slot machine he'd ever played.

I wanted to say "The building is on fire, you'd better run," but I smiled sadly and said, "You hit the jackpot. Stay put, and the attendant will be over to pay you."

I don't remember how much the man won. All I remember is that he won the jackpot that would have been mine if I'd ignored my mother and followed my instincts. Hopefully, I got some extra good karma by listening to my mother, who was totally oblivious to what had happened.

Learn to trust your own intuition when choosing and playing a machine. All the systems in the world are sometimes not as reliable as your own inner voices.

As you have surmised by now, I spend a lot of time in Laughlin, Nevada. When we first started going to Laughlin, there were just two casinos and no hotels. The hotels were on the other side of the river in Bullhead City, Arizona. There were small boats that took you back and forth across the river. Today Laughlin has its own mini strip lined with hotels and casinos. It can't compare with Las Vegas in size or glitz, but it's a good place to gamble. Like the play the favorite to show system, it's low key and sensible. The hotel rates are very inexpensive, and its proximity to the Colorado River makes it popular with families.

The Regency was one of the original casinos in Laughlin. It was a dinky place that became sandwiched between two high-rise hotels with big casinos and fancy machines. One night as we were passing by it, I felt the urge to go inside.

"Let's try this place," I said to the group of friends I was with.

"It looks like a dump," someone replied.

"Right," I agreed. "Since it doesn't have anything else to offer, the machines will have to pay better."

The inside of the Regency was dark and sparse. It reminded me of the neighborhood bars in Chicago, where I grew up. One wall was lined with the oldest Keno machines I'd ever seen, and the slot machines and video poker machines weren't much newer.

You guessed it. All of us walked out of the Regency winners because those old, no-frill machines did pay better than the new, sleek ones in the big casinos. I'm not trying to impress you with my deductive powers; I'm just suggesting that, when you're in an area that has a number of casinos, you may do well to try some of the less attractive ones.

People flock into the Bellagio or the Venetian and are surrounded by luxury. The casinos are golden, and the machines are state of the art. In order to compete with these high-profile places, the smaller casinos may have to improve the gambling odds for their patrons. That's not to say you can't win in a glitzy casino or will win in a place with less glamour. It's simply another one of my opinions based on prior experience.

Be aware of your surroundings. Become a discriminating gambler. Realize that every new casino provides competition for all the others. And, if there is only one casino in your area, take the time to learn about the video poker machines it offers.

Last year my husband and I went on a cruise with our friends Dave and Jane. The ship had one casino, and hearing the squeals of a big winner wasn't a common occurrence there.

The first time I went into the casino was a research mission. I looked at all the video poker machines, playing them sparingly and conservatively. I also observed other people playing the video poker games. Since the casino wasn't big, it didn't take me long to determine that the best-paying video poker machines were built into the bar. I don't mind a cocktail or two when I'm gambling, so this was fine with me.

Since there were many other amusements on the ship, I didn't spend a lot of time in the casino, but when I did go in there to gamble I always walked out a winner. That was because I'd taken the time to check things out and find the video poker machines that dealt out winning hands consistently.

On my last visit to Laughlin, the Regency casino was closed. It's probably going to be torn down and replaced by another high-rise hotel/casino. I'm sure the new place will be very nice, and it may even become one of my regular gambling spots, but I'll miss the Regency and that old video poker machine that dealt out nice winning hands more often than not.

CHAPTER 17

Final Review

Video poker is one of the most popular casino games, and with each new machine and each new variation it becomes more fascinating and entertaining. One of the best things about playing video poker is that it requires some skill and concentration. Unlike many slot machines, which don't require anything but the ability to push buttons or pull handles, video poker presents an opportunity to compete, a chance to match your wits against the computerized game. The best way to do this is not by playing faster but by playing smarter. It's accomplished by developing the ability to analyze each deal and determine the most advantageous way to play the hand. The basics of poker are simple and can be learned by most people, and the game can be adapted to a number of different formats and varieties.

My uncles thought that calling one-eyed kings wild on a given hand was the ultimate in cleverness. I often wonder what they'd think of the sleek, colorful video poker machines that allow you to play five, 10, 50, or even 100 hands at once. They might say that playing poker with people is more fun than playing against a machine. I'd say that depends on the people you are playing against.

Our family poker games were wonderful because they were friendly and filled with crazy antics and laughter. No one took the games too seriously. I'm sure there are still many people who play poker that way. There are also many people who take poker very seriously. When you sit at their tables, you play by established rules; you can't make them up just because it's your turn to deal.

While video poker machines don't allow you to make up your own rules or hands either, they do allow you to play the game in your own way and at your own speed. Even the phantom dealer on the Odyssey machine who cracks his knuckles and drums his fingers when you take too long to hold and discard is there just to enhance the game for the player.

Video poker machines are designed to keep the player interested so that the money keeps flowing into them. The manufacturers are always developing new gimmicks and new variations on the game in order to attract more and more people to the computerized machines.

A live poker game can become stressful depending on

who is playing and how high the stakes are. With video poker, you control the stakes, and, if you are playing sensibly and skillfully, it should be relaxing and amusing.

Computers have simplified our lives in countless ways and given us the tools to reach across the world. We use them for communication. We use them for research. It's only fitting that they can also be used for entertainment.

There are no clocks in casinos. The casino operators want you to forget about time and stay as long as possible. They are hoping, of course, that you will spend that time losing your money. I'd also like readers of this book to stay in the casino as long as possible. The difference is that I want you to stay there because you are having a good time and not losing your money. Playing video poker should be fun. It should be as enjoyable as those family poker games that made our house ring with laughter.

All the video poker games covered in this book can be found in most casinos and can be played using the play the favorite to show method. When played sensibly and conservatively, these games will provide you with hours of enjoyment. Gambling can be a pleasant diversion from the trials and tribulations of everyday life. Of course, your level of enjoyment will also be measured by the amount of cash your video poker sessions produce.

Let's take a last look at the games covered in this book and review how they can be played to achieve the highest level of entertainment.

Jacks or Better, five-card draw, video poker can be found on both nickel and quarter machines. Play the maximum on nickel machines and the minimum on quarter machines. When you approach a quarter machine, look at the payout schedule and ask yourself this question: "If I hit the royal flush, will I be happy with the payout amount for a one-coin bet?" Remember that, on most quarter machines, the top payout for a one-coin bet amounts to about $65. Recall the earlier chart showing that the payouts for a bet of one quarter and a bet of five nickels are the same except for the royal flush jackpot. Also remember that the royal flush comes up only once in every 44,000 hands. Yet the last hand played on that machine could have been 43,999, so the machine could be ready to deal you a royal flush.

If you answer yes to the above question, sit down and play the machine. If you answer no, either play more coins or move to a nickel machine. The top payout on a nickel machine for a royal flush is 4,000 coins or $200. Whether you play a nickel machine or a quarter machine, you should always be looking for the smaller, more consistent wins.

The following table will remind you what you should be holding and discarding.

Hand to Hold	Cards Held	Cards Drawn
Royal flush	5	0
Straight flush	5	0
Four of a kind	4	1
Full house	5	0
Flush	5	0
Three of a kind	3	2
Straight	5	0
Four to a straight flush	4	1
Two pair	4	1
Four to a flush	4	1
High pair	2	3
Four to a straight	4	1
Low pair	2	3
Three to a straight flush	3	2
Three to a straight	3	2
Three to a royal flush	3	2
One face card	1	4
Two face cards	2	3
Two to a royal flush	2	3
None of the above	0	5

The table lists the biggest winning hands first, although you don't need to be told to hold any of those hands if you are lucky enough to have one of them dealt to you.

The most important part of the table is the order in which other deals should be played. Note that four to a flush is given a higher preference than a high pair. This is strictly a judgment call, one of those times when you may want to use your psychic powers to help you decide. Although a flush pays more, a high pair of jacks or better is an automatic win. The same goes for four to a straight, especially if you aren't trying to fill an inside straight. The fact that you have decisions to make when playing video poker is what sets this game apart from other gaming machines.

Unless I have built up a substantial number of credits over my initial investment, I usually go for the sure win of a high pair over four to a flush or four to a straight. This is probably because of the many times I've been dealt four to a flush or a straight and then failed to get the fifth card to complete the win. As you've already learned, it's better to collect on a lesser win than to lose your bet trying to get a higher payout.

Multiple-play video poker machines give you a chance to play from three to 100 hands of poker at once. They usually have more than one poker game that can be selected and played on the machine. They also have a range of coin denominations that can be selected.

Don't forget to check out the payout schedules for each game, and choose the one that has the most generous payouts. Also remember that, the more hands you play, the bigger your risk. Sitting at a multiple-hand machine doesn't mean that you have to play all the hands. You can always reduce your risk by playing fewer hands or playing a lower coin denomination. No matter how many hands you are playing, keep your focus. The first hand dealt is the one you must study. If you have an automatic win on that hand, hold it and collect on all the hands being played.

Almost wins on multiple-play machines are good since you have all those extra hands and decks of cards to try to complete the win.

Avoid using the turbo play button or icon to speed up the deals. Playing faster won't help you to win more.

The Odyssey has a video poker game with a phantom dealer. The graphics are great and make the game fun to play. I love to play this particular machine; however, because it's a quarter machine and doesn't pay out as well as the standard video poker venues, I play it cautiously, risking only the minimum amount on each hand. If you've never played video poker on an Odyssey, try it once just for the fun of it.

Someone told me recently that a manufacturer is working on a video poker game that has marvelous graphics and the ability to bluff and raise bets. I don't know if this information is accurate; if it is, though, the graphics designed for the Odyssey machines have likely been the stepping-stones to this futuristic game of video poker.

Another video poker machine is similar in design to the Odyssey. It's probably a product of the same manufacturer. This one is called Lucky Draw. I didn't cover it in previous chapters since it's just one more multiple-hand machine. Lucky Draw has four hands to play and is usually a quarter machine. I've played the machines with some success, but, like the Odyssey, they don't pay as well as standard video poker machines.

Double Down machines aren't as popular as they once were, but they can still be found on the casino floor. The only thing you need to remember about Double Down is that it's designed to let you win more on the initial hands. If you take those wins and aren't tempted to risk them on the Double Down segment of the game, you'll come out ahead. These are Jacks or Better machines, and the suggested system works the same on them as it does on regular Jacks or Better machines.

Spin Poker machines are noisy and fun to play. But I think they are somewhat of a novelty on the casino floor. If you're simply looking for a change of pace, Spin Poker will provide that. I've seen people win substantial amounts on Spin Poker, usually when they are playing Deuces Wild and sometimes when they are betting several coins per line. Given the choice between Spin Poker and a Hundred Play video poker machine, I'd choose Spin Poker, but only if there were no regular Jacks or Better single-play machines available.

Four of a Kind video poker machines are usually plentiful. In keeping with their name, the payout schedules can be quite generous for four of a kind wins, especially if you hit four aces. Most of these are quarter machines, although there are some older nickel machines around. Actually, these machines are just Jacks or Better poker machines and should be played in the same way. The nice thing about Four of a Kind machines is that you can collect 160 coins for one coin bet on some hands. In other words, you can play the minimum of one quarter and get a hefty payout.

When choosing between quarter and nickel machines, keep in mind that there are 40 coins in a roll of nickels and 40 coins in a roll of quarters, but a roll of nickels is worth two dollars, while a roll of quarters is worth $10.

Sometimes video poker machines need to be nursed along a bit before they slip into a winning cycle. With nickels, you can afford to play the maximum and give the machine time to kick into a winning cycle. With quarters, it's prudent to play one at a time until you see whether the machine is going to start giving you a good return on your investment.

Sneak Peek video poker is another game that doesn't appeal to a large segment of casino gamblers. I like this game because, by getting a look at my next draw card, I can adjust an almost win hand that isn't going to materialize and salvage my bet.

Progressive video poker machines tempt players by displaying a large jackpot in lights over the machines. But remember that the jackpot is accumulated over time by a percentage of the coins put into the machines connected to it. That means the odds of winning on those machines are slightly reduced. Also, once the jackpot reaches a certain point, professional gamblers move in and try to win it. To win a progressive jackpot, you must pay the maximum amount, and doing so increases your risk. You could get lucky and win the jackpot, but the odds aren't in your favor. That factor, coupled with the higher amount that must be bet on each hand, makes progressive games a bad choice for sensible, conservative players.

One of the newer video poker machines is called Multi-Strike. This machine could make me abandon the Odyssey. It rewards you for winning by letting you move up to the next hand, which pays double the amount the last hand paid out. I still believe that, when a new game is introduced, the initial machines are set to pay out more to get people hooked. This could be the case with Multi-Strike. However, like the Odyssey, if you've never played one, it's worth trying at least once just for the fun of it.

The hold-and-draw table doesn't apply to Deuces Wild. This isn't a Jacks or Better poker venue. A minimum win on Deuces Wild is three of a kind. Deuces are very valuable and should always be held. A pair has the potential to turn into three of a kind, so those cards should also always be held. If your initial deal doesn't yield a deuce or a pair or an almost win, it's usually better to discard it and get five new cards. In some ways, Deuces Wild is more difficult than Jacks or Better poker since you always have to decide how a wild card could fit into the cards to produce a winning hand and hold and discard accordingly.

I hope readers have absorbed and taken to heart the most important message of this book. Gambling should be fun. It's a form of recreation. It's not a way to earn the rent money, and the rent money should never be put at risk. Develop a budget for video poker that won't jeopardize your lifestyle, and find a game that you really enjoy playing.

Most casinos have a social atmosphere. Everyone is there to try his or her luck at the games. This serves as a common bond that brings people from all backgrounds and all walks of life together. Relax and enjoy the people and the excitement of the games.

You are there to have fun, and, the longer you can play a game that amuses you, the more fun you will have. You don't have to win a jackpot or even double your money; just staying ahead of the game is a testament to your skill and ingenuity. Some days you may not be able to do that, but for the most part, using the play the favorite to show system, you'll be able to meet the challenges of the games and win on a regular basis.

Winning more is the same as losing less. Losing less means you are winning more. The terms are interchangeable. No matter how you look at it, the whole idea is to get the maximum amount of enjoyment from a minimum amount of money.

Study the payout charts reviewed in this book for the various games. Doing so will give you an idea of which machines to seek out and play on your next visit to the casino.

An overview of several different video poker games has been presented. Perhaps you always play the same video poker game, or perhaps, like me, you enjoy playing all the different versions. Even if you've never played video poker before, you should now be able to sit down at a machine and play it with confidence. Try different games to see which one you enjoy the most.

Remember two key things. First, no matter how much you enjoy playing a particular game, don't let the machine take all your credits. If the machine isn't paying, and some just don't regardless of how skillfully or conservatively you are playing, cash out and move to another machine. Second, when you do win, hang on to your winnings. Don't give them back to the casino. Be aware of the winning and losing cycles that all video poker machines go through. Keep your eye on your credits and set limits.

Don't walk into a casino expecting to win a bundle. Do walk into a casino intending to win. Your mind-set is important. Think positively, keep your focus, and don't be led astray by the gimmicks that exist to make you risk more.

When you walk out of the casino, you should feel good about the time you just spent there. For people who like to gamble, it's the ultimate playground. Have fun!